WORDS-
From Print to Meaning

Lou E. Burmeister
The University of Texas at El Paso

→WORDS-
From Print to Meaning
Classroom Activities
For Building Sight Vocabulary,
For Using Context Clues,
Morphology, and Phonics

ADDISON-WESLEY PUBLISHING COMPANY
Reading, Massachusetts • Menlo Park, California
London • Amsterdam • Don Mills, Ontario • Sydney

This book is in the
ADDISON-WESLEY SERIES IN EDUCATION

ISBN 0-201-00770-3
CDEFGHIJ-AL-79

To my father and Michelle

Preface

This book has been written for preservice and inservice teachers to explain basic theory of modern traditional word analysis programs and to supply suggestions and guidelines for classwide and small group instruction in the various components of word analysis. This book is basically a handbook, and the activities outlined are meant, in most cases, to supplement a well-structured word analysis program. In some cases the explanations and activities may help the advanced reader structure his own program for individuals or groups of students.

It is important that the reader keep in mind the many facets of word analysis. The best modern programs strive for a balance by coordinating the five components of word analysis—sight vocabulary, the use of context clues, morphology, phonics, and the dictionary—and thus help the student achieve the versatility which will help make him a competent reader.

Some words of caution must accompany a book such as this:

1. Word analysis, or decoding, though basic to reading is only a small part of the total reading act. Without word analysis skills a person cannot read, but reading involves much more than word analysis. Basic to reading is the derivation of meaning from the author's symbols, as such meaning relates to the background of experience of the reader, the reaction of the reader to this meaning, and the integration of the meaning with what the reader already knows about the subject. In accord with the meaning emphasis point of view, the activities suggested in this book deal not only

with breaking the code, but also with achieving understanding at levels possible in a word analysis program.

2. Word analysis games, as well as other word analysis activities, can be overdone in the classroom. The teacher should always have a specific reason for selecting a game or activity for use with students.

3. In the English-speaking world there are vast dialectical differences. A modern reading word analysis program, especially a phonics program, is not designed to "correct" a student's oral English. Rather, it is designed principally to help the student recognize relationships between the printed symbols he sees and the oral counterpart which he probably knows. Such a relationship will differ from area to area even in the United States—and often even within a community.

In line with the principle of *descriptive* linguistics, a word analysis, especially a phonics, program is designed to teach these relationships as they exist, not to censure the child or the dialect because pronunciations differ from those of the General American dialect. If the reader of this book is teaching children who have dialects other than General American, some adjustments will be necessary.

This book contains four very practical chapters, plus an introduction. The introductory chapter is designed to give the reader definitions of important terminology and a framework, or structure, for a total word analysis program. Some readers may prefer to examine this chapter only briefly before studying the remainder of the book and to come back to it as a summary chapter after being fortified with examples. Others may wish to grasp the framework at the onset before looking at the practical applications suggested in Chapters 1 through 4. Either of these approaches is satisfactory.

El Paso, Texas   L.E.B.
February 1975

Contents

Introduction

Reading specialists commonly talk about five word attack, word identification, or word recognition skills. In a hierarchical listing of these—starting with the one that is least time-consuming—are:

1. sight recognition
2. context clues
3. morphology (structural analysis)
4. phonics
5. dictionary use

DEFINITIONS OF WORD ATTACK SKILLS

By *sight recognition* is meant the recognition of a word or phrase by a quick gestalt. Clues used are the distinctive shape of the word or phrase and/or some letters. Words recognized in this way, obviously, must have been seen at least once before in print and attacked in some other way that time. A word recognized at sight may or may not have meaning for the reader.

The utilization of *context clues* and morphology (sometimes called structural analysis) as word attack skills deals with meaning. Among the more common types of context clues are: *real objects* (a real object may be labeled—as a piñata, a blowfish, a tetrahedron, a daffodil); *pictures* (a picture of a piñata, a blowfish, a tetrahedron, a daffodil may be labeled); *experiences* (former or present observations may be a clue to a word in a sentence, such as "The American flag is red, white, and _____ ."); *words, sentences, or paragraphs* themselves may supply the experiences necessary to get the meaning, though not the pronunciation, of a new word (e.g., "Just before sunset the majestic mountains were a purplish-blue—the color an artist would call *mauve*". . . or, "A chill went up her spine—there was a scratching on the window screen. It was dark, and she was alone and afraid. What an *eerie* feeling she had.") Common sentence patterns may also supply clues, as in "Ozzie went ____ the ball park."

Morphology, as a word attack skill, deals with the recognition of meaningful parts, or morphemes, which compose words. Morphemes are the smallest meaning units of our language and may be *free*, as are words, or *bound*, as are prefixes, some roots, and suffixes. A reader using morphology (or structural analysis) may know the free English morpheme *kind* and the bound morpheme *un-*, as in *unlike, unable, unnecessary*. When he first meets *unkind* in his reading, he should find it a simple task to induce the meaning of that word. The same is true for a more advanced student who knows *tele-* from *telephone, telegraph*, and *teletype* and *-pathy* from *sympathy, apathy*, and *empathy* to arrive at the meaning of *telepathy*.

Phonics is an altogether different type of word attack skill, for it deals with relationships between printed symbols and sounds, not meanings. Phonics will be of no help to the reader interested in getting meaning unless he orally knows the word being attacked. Researchers commonly talk about paired associates. It might be helpful to think of phonics as part of a *triple-associate* skill. The printed symbol triggers the sound (paired level), and the sound triggers the meaning (triple-associate level). For example, the reader sees the word *cat*; he responds orally /kăt/; he remembers that sound to be the oral symbol for a fluffy, four-legged animal with a tail—or for the woman who scratches and claws. Unless the triple-associate relationship is present, utilizing phonic skills can be busywork.

Using a *dictionary* for the purpose of word identification is often a last resort. If the reader cannot understand a word by using one of the above techniques, finding it in a dictionary will help. However, such a task is time consuming and probably ought to be reserved for the most difficult words.

Some Criticisms Considered

Some linguists criticize reading teachers for attempting to teach children to use what these linguists consider to be diametrically opposite types of word attack skills. They argue that children might be taught either sight recognition or phonics (or an alphabetic decoding system such as Bloomfield's or Fries'), *but not both.* Note the following statement: "It has not seemed to occur to most of these teachers and authors that, quite obviously, the phonics and whole-word approaches are polar opposites, and if one is correct the other must be wrong, and 'eclectic' approach must mean that at least part of the time the teaching is based on faulty premises which can only increase the confusion of the learner."[1]

It is difficult for reading experts to understand such criticism, for reading people have long felt that a flexible approach is desirable. Some words can be recognized at sight easily—those that are meaningful to the reader, those that have distinctive shapes, and those that the reader has seen often in print. The independent reader must somehow attack other words—including each word he is seeing in print for the first time.

Then why not count on *just phonics* and not sight at all? Because phonics doesn't always work, and it is time consuming. Although it is fine to use phonics clues when necessary, constant use of phonics leads to tediousness in reading.

Does anyone criticize the young mathematician for recognizing a rectangle at a glance but for having to count the sides of another figure before he knows it's a decagon? Does anyone criticize the budding poet for recognizing blank verse to be that—at a glance—but for having to scan another stanza before he knows it is trochee pentameter? Or, does anyone criticize the botanist who knows a cypress at first view but must induce that a certain flower is a frangipani that he's read about in a book but has never seen before? If not, then why are readers criticized for using various types of word recognition clues?

---

[1] H.L. Smith, Jr., *English Morphophonics: Implications for the Teaching of Literacy,* SUNY at Oneonta, New York: New York State English Council, 1968, p.1.

CONTENT OF A PHONICS PROGRAM

Former Objections to Content of Programs

For a long time teachers and children have felt overburdened with vast numbers of phonics generalizations. Many of these "generalizations" had *limited usefulness*, in that they applied to only a few words that the children read. Others were *invalid*, in that there were more exceptions to the generalizations than there were instances of application. When being queried by an observant youngster, the teacher too frequently repeated, "That word, Hortense, is an exception to the generalization."

The thousands of Hortenses and Freds led several reading researchers to supply objective evidence to publishers and teachers that, indeed, our phonics programs had gone far astray (Clymer,[2] Bailey,[3] Emans,[4] Burmeister[5]). Such evidence gave impetus to the growing demand for revised programs.

There are two possible logical effects of the recognition that many of our generalizations are limited in usefulness and/or validity. One effect might be that the teaching of phonics would be almost eliminated from our reading programs. Another effect might be that researchers examine the language—linguistically—in search of generalizations which are truly descriptive of modern English.

Content Components of a Modern Phonics Program—Introduction

In essence, there has been a complementary trend in both directions. First, it is now felt that there is a need to teach fewer generalizations than were taught in the past. And, second, some generalizations have been revised to gain greater validity. We describe grapheme to phoneme (written symbol to sound) relation-

---

[2] Theodore L. Clymer, "The Utility of Phonic Generalizations in the Primary Grades," *The Reading Teacher* 16 (January 1963): 252-258.

[3] Mildred Hart Bailey, "The Utility of Phonic Generalizations in Grades One through Six," *The Reading Teacher* 20 (February 1967): 413-418.

[4] Robert Emans, "The Usefulness of Phonic Generalizations above the Primary Grades," *The Reading Teacher* 20 (February 1967): 419-425.

[5] Lou E. Burmeister, "The Usefulness of Phonic Generalizations," *The Reading Teacher* 21(January 1968): 349-346; and "Selected Word Analysis Generalizations for a Group Approach to Corrective Reading in the Secondary School," *Reading Research Quarterly* IV(Fall 1968): 71-95.

ships *within morphemes* (meaningful parts of words) for the following situations:

1. Consonants
    a)   single consonants (b, c, d, f, etc.)
    b)   consonant blends (bl, cl, dr, sm, spl, etc.)
    c)   consonant digraphs (ph, sh, ch, th, ng)
    d)   silent consonants (-mb, -lm; wr-, kn-, etc., and one of two consecutive like consonants, e.g., ba*ll*oon, ra*bb*it)
2. Vowels
    a)   single vowels (a, e, i, o, u, y)
    b)   final *single* vowel-consonant-e (-ape, ice, etc.)
    c)   vowel clusters (ai, oa, oi, ou, ei, etc.)
    d)   the r control (*c*ar, h*er*, h*ear*, *c*are, etc.)
    e)   "consonantizing" of *i* in the following situations: *-tio, -tia, -cio, -cia, -sio* (mansion, action, vision, fusion, caution, etc.)
3. Phonic syllabication in the following patterns:
    a)   vowel-consonant-consonant-vowel (aster, silver)
    b)   vowel-consonant-vowel (razor , lemon)
    c)   final consonant-l-e (maple, cable)

En toto, then , there are twelve categories that need to be covered in a phonics program—not really very many! Each of these will be more thoroughly discussed in Chapter 3.[6]

SCOPE AND ORGANIZATION OF THIS BOOK

This book has been written to give teachers and prospective teachers a basic understanding of three of the components of a modern word analysis program—context clues, morphology, and phonics—with some discussion of sight vocabulary. The book has been designed to be practical, rather than theoretical—with explanations at a minimum, but examples for classroom practice stressed. Chapter 3, however, deals with the content of a phonics program because it is felt that most teachers need a thorough

---

[6] Please see Appendixes D and E for representative sequential patterns used in teaching these components.

explanation of phonic principles which are worth teaching. Classwide and small-group activities for teaching these principles are found in Chapter 4.

No attempt is made to discuss in detail basic phonic methodology, partly because there are so many valid, though sometimes conflicting, methods for teaching phonic skills. This book would become a tome if all these were considered. It is suggested that the reader of this book carefully examine one, or several, commercial phonics-based programs after completing the chapters on phonics in this book.[7] The activities described in Chapter 4 are meant to supplement such a program, chiefly in the primary grades.

Nevertheless, in Chapter 3, titled "Content of a Phonics Program," there are some thorough explanations of recommended basic classroom practice. These explanations are designed to show the teacher of students at the fourth-grade level, or above, how to teach certain phonics lessons in a mature way. There are too few commercial materials which successfully do this. These procedures are included also to help the reader of this book better understand the principles. Several research studies have indicated that teachers and prospective teachers, themselves, do not know these principles.

Chapter by Chapter Organization

Chapter 1 of this book deals with ways of utilizing *context clues* to help children both develop their vocabularies and identify new words and, ideally, to transfer many of these words to their sight vocabularies. This should be an ongoing process. Additionally, in this chapter some activities are suggested to introduce phonics in its simplest forms to children by combining the use of context clues with specific phonics elements.

Chapter 2 deals with ways of making the teaching of *morphology* both interesting and meaningful.

Chapter 3 concerns itself chiefly with the content of a modern *phonics* program—with some discussion of methods of teaching phonics, as explained earlier.

Chapter 4 includes suggested classwide, group, and individual activities useful in the teaching of *phonics* to children.

This book has been written for teachers and prospective teachers of children in the primary and middle grades. Teachers of students in secondary schools may find some parts of this book helpful, particularly in working with problem readers.

---

[7] See Appendix D for a list of suggested programs.

Utilizing
Context Clues

Jamie sits on his mother's lap as she reads a story to him. It's a
familiar tale, and as she proceeds, he gleefully points to words and
says them: "Rumpelstiltskin" ... "name" ... "spin" ... Jamie
has heard this story before, and these words have been pointed out
to him.

Chapter 1

Another day, Jamie retrieves the daily newspaper from behind
the shrubs. He brings it indoors and points to a headline:
"RAILROAD STRIKE." He says, "railroad." He's learned that
word in caps because a few blocks from home there's a track, next
to which is a sign on the road: "RAILROAD." All the children
can read that sign, and Jamie can read it even out of that context.

When watching TV, Jamie can pick out such words as
"Coca-Cola," "Pepsi," "Kellogg's," "Ultra Brite." And, along the
way, he's even learned his A, B, C's.

Thus Jamie, like thousands of other children, enters school
already knowing—at sight—some words and maybe all the letters.
What can his teacher do to accelerate his growth in sight
recognition and to extend his ability to independently identify
words?

Words are never recognized at sight the first time they are
seen. Some other technique must be used the first time a reader
identifies a word. Only with repetition—sometimes frequent,
sometimes rare—is a word recognized at sight.

A commonly used way of teaching children new words is by
using context clues. For example, see the following techniques.

7

EARLY STAGES

Early
Stages

□   **Names.** Letter the child's name on a card. He'll want to learn to read his own name. Pin the card on his shirt so his classmates will learn it too. Do this for all the children, and soon most will be able to read the names of all the children in the class. When the children can read the names on the cards without having them pinned on the child, they are said to know the words by *sight*.

□   **Objects in the Room.** Label objects in the classroom with their names. Put corresponding words in a WORD BANK, a box with a hole in it large enough so that the child can insert his hand to "draw out" a card. When time permits, ask each child in order to take a card, using a "spelldown" technique. Ask the child to read the word. (If he can read the word, it is probably in his *sight* vocabulary.) If he can't read it, send him around the room to match the card with a like card on the object, and then ask him to read it. (The object is the context clue.)

The child's team gets two points if the child reads the card without matching it with the card on the object, one point if he matches it and says it, and zero points if he can do neither, in which case the card goes to the other team. A failing response should not result in the child being asked to sit down. He remains in the game. The team with the highest score wins.

□   **Child's Choice.** Ask each child what word he wants to learn to read. When a child tells you his or her word, print it on the bottom of a 3 X 5" card.

pumpkin

Next, ask the child to illustrate it.

pumpkin

Next, cut the card like a jigsaw puzzle.

pumpkin

After the child has a few cards, cut another 3 × 5" card into five
3 × 1" rectangular pieces. Print each word on one of these cards,
thus:

pumpkin   witch   Hallowe'en

mask   Susan   etc.

Each of these smaller cards has as a counterpart the 3 × 5" card
made into a jigsaw puzzle with the word on one part and its illustration on the other.

The child can put a rubber band around his set of 3 × 1"
cards. When he tries to read one and cannot, he should match the
card with the corresponding word which is part of the jigsaw
puzzle card, thus:

pumpkin   Hallowe'en   witch

mask   Susan   witch

Next he matches the jigsaw card with the illustration and should
then know the word.

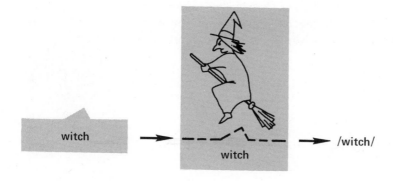

witch → witch → /witch/

LANGUAGE EXPERIENCE APPROACH

☐ **The Language Experience Approach.** The language experience approach is usually exciting for children. After the children have observed something which to them is interesting, they may dictate a sentence, or possibly even a story, to the teacher. In its simplest form, the teacher might simply write a sentence which the child has spoken, for example:

Language Experience

Terry pulled the gerbil's tail.

The teacher would point to the sentence, going from left to right as she reads it. The child is asked to read along with her. He would, thus, read the whole sentence, although he might not know any individual word in it.

Following this, the teacher would copy the sentence on a piece of heavy paper and cut it into phrases or word groups:

Terry pulled   the gerbil's tail.

She would then teach the child to read each of these word groups. Next she would jumble them and ask him to arrange them in left-to-right order on his desk, in a pocket chart, or in the chalk trough.

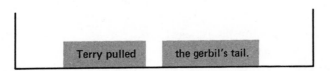

Then she would cut the "word groups" into separate words. Then she would teach the child each word individually, shuffle all of them, and then ask him to arrange them in left-to-right order:

Terry   pulled   the   gerbil's   tail.

If a group of children are working together on this, the teacher might distribute each card to a different child. The children, then, would line up from left to right:

☐ **CLOZE Technique (Word Substitution).** Continuing this, she might use a CLOZE technique, taking out a word and asking the child to suggest words in place of the word removed. For example:

1. Terry pulled the   gerbil's   tail.
   Terry pulled the   _____'s   tail.
   Terry pulled the   monkey's   tail.
   Terry pulled the   elephant's   tail.
   Terry pulled the   cat's   tail.
   Terry pulled the   hippo's   tail.

2. Terry pulled the   gerbil's   _____.
                                      hair
                                      foot

3. Terry _____ the gerbil's tail.
         twisted
         petted

4. _____ pulled the gerbil's tail.
   Lorna
   Henry
   Jackie

☐ **Introducing Phonic Elements.** In another sentence, such as the following,

   I wish I had a dog. —or— I wish I had a ball.

the teacher might ask students to supply words which begin with the same sound as "dog" or "ball":

   I wish I had a d_____ .   I wish I had a b_____.

They might suggest:

I wish I had a d_____.   I wish I had a b_____.

        dinosaur   bat
        doughnut   bicycle
        dinghy   book
        duck   banana

Language Experience

After writing these on the board, the teacher would point out that all the words in the same group sound the same at the beginning, and they all are spelled with the same letter—"d" (or "b"). Thus she would be teaching a simple phonics lesson.

☐   **Classifying.** After several, or many, words of real interest to the children are suggested in activities such as the above, print each of these words on a 3 × 5" card. Suggest to children that they sort these words in various ways, e.g., according to:

initial letters
final letters
vowels
things they like best
things they like least
etc.

Ask them to suggest categories for classifying the words. If pictures are available, ask children to match words with appropriate pictures.

LINGUISTIC APPROACHES

☐   **Sentence Approach.** The teacher might choose, in addition, or instead, to use a linguistic approach. One particularly interesting approach is the sentence approach.

According to C. C. Fries[1], the English language is one of a few languages in which one can compose sentences using nonsense words for all (or most) words other than signal words and still know the parts of speech of the nonsense words. For example, in the sentence:

The iggle wogs an uggle.[2]

we know that "iggle" is a noun (subject), "wogs" is the verb, and "uggle" is the predicate noun. We also know that the iggle is acting upon the uggle.

What parts of speech are the nonsense words in the following sentences:

The uggle is wogged by the iggle.

The uggle is vemp.

Since in English it can be argued that word order is such a strong clue to parts of speech and, therefore, to meaning, it can also be argued that a sentence approach is a valid and very desirable approach to teaching oral language (for ESL programs) and reading.

Carl Lefevre identifies only four basic patterns of English sentences:[3]

Pattern I:	N V	Terry plays.
	N V Ad	Terry plays well.
Pattern II:	N V N	Terry caught the ball.
Pattern III:	N V N N	Terry gave Rover a bone.
	N V N A	Terry made Rover happy.

---

[1] C.C. Fries, *Linguistics and Reading*, New York: Holt, Rinehart, and Winston, 1963, pp. 72, 105-106.

[2] Signal words *the* and *an* are noun signal words, or noun markers, i.e., they tell us a noun is coming. Noun markers are initial words in noun phrases.

[3] Carl Lefevre, *Linguistics and the Teaching of Reading*, New York: McGraw-Hill, 1964, pp. 84-91.

Pattern IV: N Lv N   Terry is my name (or, My name is Terry.)

N Lv A   Terry is angry.

N Lv Ad   Terry is here.

In a reading program, the teacher might select a pattern, teach it thoroughly, and then move on to another pattern, etc.

Linguistic Approaches

1. For example, one might begin with pattern IV (N Lv N) thus:

a) My name is Terry.   (What is your name?)

My name is _____.   (What is your name?)

My name is Joan.

My name is Juanita.

My name is Robert.

b) Cloze both nouns:

My _____   is _____.

My game   is baseball.   (What is your game?)

My game   is hopscotch. (What is your game?)

My game   is football.

My game   is jacks.

My game   is rummy.

c) Cloze the verb:

My game   _____   rummy.

My game   was   rummy.

My game   will be   rummy.

2. Try pattern IV (N Lv A) thus:

a) Terry is angry.

_____   is _____.

Joan   is happy.

Juanita is sad.

Robert   is kind.

Robert   _____   kind.

Robert   was   kind.

Robert   will be   kind.

b) The candy is good.

Add elaborations: The ∧ candy is good.

i.e.: The _____ candy is good.

kind: The peppermint candy is good.

The chocolate candy is good.

Add elaborations: The ∧ chocolate candy is good.

i.e.: The _____ chocolate candy is good.

kind: The milk chocolate candy is good.

The bitter chocolate candy is good.

color: The dark chocolate candy is good.

The pastel chocolate candy is good.

Add elaborations: The pastel chocolate candy ∧ is good.

i.e.: The pastel chocolate candy _____ is good.

from whom: The pastel chocolate candy from grandma is good.

3. Pattern I (N V) might be used thus:

a) Terry plays.   Terry is playing.

Terry _____ s.   Terry is _____ ing.

Terry reads.   Terry is reading.

Terry sings.   Terry is singing.

Terry runs.   Terry is running.

or

The boy	is	playing.
The _____	is	playing.
The girl	is	playing.
The teacher	is	playing.
The dog	is	playing.

b) Add *single word* predicate elaborations:

The boy   is playing _____.
The boy   is playing ball.
The girl   is playing tennis.
The teacher is playing bridge.

c) Add predicate elaborations of *phrase length*:

The dog is playing _____ .
The dog is playing with a stick.

d) Cloze noun and verb:

The _____ is _____ ing.
The donkey   is braying.
The dog   is barking.
The cow   is mooing.
The cat   is meowing.

e) Add subject elaborations:

The ∧ donkey is braying.

i.e.:   The _____   donkey is braying.
        The shaggy   donkey is braying.
        The spotted   donkey is braying.

The ∧ spotted donkey is braying.

i.e.:   The _____   spotted donkey is braying.
        The small   spotted donkey is braying.

☐ **Blocks.** Use foam rubber (for silence), plastic, or wooden blocks—one for each part of speech. Each block, in fact, could be a different color. Put a suitable word on each side of each block, thus:

If you wish to use the N Lv A pattern:

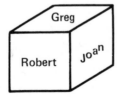
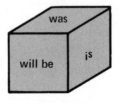
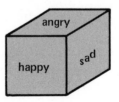

Have children toss the blocks. Using the words that are on the top, they formulate a sentence. They will note that normally the red cube goes first, followed by the blue cube, followed by the green one, although an inversion is possible, e.g., Is Greg angry?

☐ **Pocket Charts.** Instead of using blocks, or in addition, pocket charts might be used, with words and/or phrases written on slips of paper which might be inserted in the pockets, e.g.:

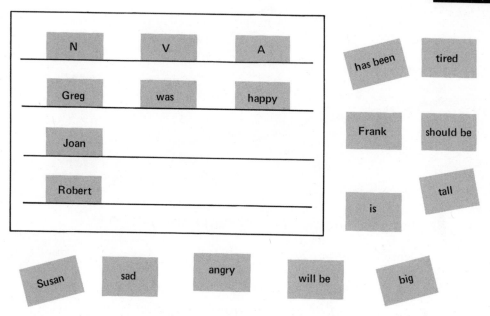

☐ **Compression.** Teach children to combine sentences. For example:

I have a ball. My ball is red.   or:
becomes: I like to read. I like to swim.
I have a red ball.   becomes:
or: I like to read and swim.
Terry has a dog. It is spotted.
becomes:
Terry has a spotted dog.

☐   **Introduce Phonic Elements.** As in the language experience approach, so, too, in a linguistic approach, it is possible to introduce phonic elements while also teaching specific sentence patterns; for example, with a N V N pattern:

1. T'is the night before Christmas, and

*B*ob wants a   b_____,   *F*red wants a   f_____.
                 baseball   football
                 boxer   fish

*D*ick wants a   d_____.   *G*retta wants a g_____.
                  dog   gown
                  dachshund
                  dinghy   *H*enry wants a h_____.
                                                   hound.

Etc.

2. Close the initial letter, thus:

*P*at wants a   __at.   *B*en wants a   __en.
                 cat   hen
                 hat   ten
                 bat   pen

Etc.

☐   **Signal Words, and Phrase or Sentence Reading.** In line with such a linguistic program, it might be noted that our "empty" words are often *signal words*; that is, they signal the beginning of a phrase or clause. They are "function" words, and perhaps are more easily and interestingly learned in context, rather than alone.

Among the most common types of signal words (*function words*, or *markers*) are (after Lefevre)[4] :

noun markers: a, an, the; one, two three . . .; these, those, etc.

verb markers: is, am, was, were, will be, has been, etc.

phrase markers: of, above, under, with, into, from, for, etc.

clause markers: however, nevertheless, since, consequently, if, etc.

question markers: who, what, when, where, why, how

---

[4]*Ibid.*, p. 19.

Each of these words commonly marks, or signals, the beginning of a phrase or clause. For example, a noun marker tells us a noun is coming, perhaps immediately or perhaps after an adjective or two. When we see the word *a*, for example, we can expect a noun phrase:

a ball	a red ball
a boy	a big boy
a game	a great game
a girl	a little girl

Linguistic
Approaches

To make the reading of these markers more interesting and meaningful than they would be if they were presented as individual words, they might be presented as the introductory word in a phrase (noun, verb, phrase markers) or a clause (clause, question markers), thus:

the _____	was _____	in _____
the kitten	was meowing	in the yard
the elephant	was dancing	in the tent
the light	was burning	in the bedroom

☐ **Intonation.** Broad context is usually the clue to intonation—and to meaning. A single sentence—alone—is often not enough to convey precise meaning. For example, demonstrate to children by emphasizing a different word each time how the meaning of the following sentence changes:

Fred didn't catch that big fish.	(Fred didn't. Someone else did.)
Fred *didn't* catch that big fish.	(Strong denial)
Fred didn't *catch* that big fish.	(Fred didn't catch it. Someone gave it to him.)
Fred didn't catch *that* big fish.	(Fred didn't catch that one. He caught another one.)
Fred didn't catch that *big* fish.	(Fred caught the little one.)
Fred didn't catch that big *fish*.	(Fred caught the big _____.)

Use sentences such as the following in the same way, emphasizing one word, then another. Ask children to explain what the paragraph might be like in each case, using this sentence as the first sentence. To add interest, children might be given cards. They come to the front of the room and stand in order to make a sentence, thus:

Linguistic
Approaches

One at a time, a child steps forward when the class is reading the sentence. The word he holds is emphasized.

1. I didn't fail the test.
2. I wish I could go to New York.
3. Sue baked the birthday cake.
4. It is John's birthday.
5. Juanita is going to college.
6. The lamp is burning.
7. My cat caught a bird.
8. Your dog broke my vase.
9. Henry's mother spanked him.
10. I want to go to the zoo.

MISCELLANEOUS ACTIVITIES

☐   **Analogies.** Have children complete analogies. For example:
Black is to *white* as *tall* is to_____.
Man is to *woman* as *boy* is to_____.
Ham is to *pig* as_____ is to *deer*.

When analogies are used, sometimes there are several possible word choices.

☐   **Similes.** Have children complete similes:

As warm as   _____
              _____
              _____

As soft as   _____
              _____
              _____

As green as   _____
              _____
              _____

As pretty as _____
              _____
              _____

Etc.

Miscellaneous

☐   **In What Context Do These Words Belong?** List about 12 – 20 words on the board. Ask the children to designate family names, or concepts, by which some of them might be classified. To go beyond the obvious, don't stop until there are at least twelve or more concepts given.

For example:

green	orange	yellow	purple
blue	pink	white	red
rose	black	fushia	lime
lemon	tan	tangerine	beige

Concept	Items	Additional Items
1. citrus fruits	orange, lime, lemon, tangerine	grapefruit
2. flowers	rose, pink, fushia	
3. words with connotations	green, blue, lemon, pink, red, yellow, etc.	
4. etc.		

Miscellaneous

☐ **Punctuation Makes a Difference.** To show children that punctuation does matter, use sentences such as the following. Ask them how the sentence meaning changes with the change in punctuation.

1. The teacher said Harry was wrong.

   "The teacher," said Harry, "was wrong."

2. "Mary," said Betty, "likes chocolates."

   Mary said Betty likes chocolates.

3. Henry Hamilton, Mary Louise John, and my cousin Beulah went.

   Henry, Hamilton, Mary Louise, John, and my cousin Beulah went.

   Henry, Hamilton, Mary, Louise, John, and my cousin Beulah went.

☐ **Short Passages and the CLOZE Technique.** Compose passages containing several sentences, such as those below, leaving blanks to be filled in. Distribute the same passage to each child in a group, and ask each to fill in the blanks. After completing their work, have the children share what they have written. Point out to them that different endings were necessary because each child filled in different words at the beginning, e.g.:

1. It was a (an) _____ day, a day for _____.
   As I went to _____, I knew what was about to happen. And it did! My best friend had _____.

2. We had just arrived at _____. With us we brought _____
   _____. My _____ said, "_____
   _____." She (He) was _____
   _____. We had _____.

☐ **Words with Multiple Meanings.** Ask children to write as many sentences as they can, using the word *run* (in any form—run, running, runs, etc.), but each time using it with a different meaning. Give them about five minutes. (Other words with multiple meanings could be used at other times.)

Then ask the children to count off: 1, 2, 3, 4, 5,. . . . 1, 2, 3, 4, 5,. . . .etc. All the one's go in one group, the two's in another, etc.

A representative from each group, in order, is asked to give a sentence using the word *run* in a way it has not been used before. The first time around, each correct response is worth one point, the second time around, two points, etc. (As the activity continues, the children may, of course, compose new sentences. They are not limited to the use of those written before.)

Miscellaneous

The children, themselves, serve as umpires. So they must listen to the contributions of all groups. The team with the highest score wins.

☐ **Tired Words.** Proceed as in the above game, except that the children must substitute words for a tired word, such as "said," or for an idea, such as "the way a person might move from point *A* to point *B*." The substituted word should be part of a phrase or sentence. For example:

He *growled*, "Get out of my way."

He *cheered*, "Yea for our side."

They *buzzed*, "This seems like nonsense."

Etc.

or

Betty *strutted* across the room.

Henry *sashayed* down the corridor.

Mary *tripped* through the tulips.

John *galloped* out to the ball park.

Etc.

A scribe might list all words that are suggested, and this list might be reproduced on the board, or children might be given individual copies. Then children might be asked to classify the words, as in the activity titled "In What Context Do These Words Belong?" above. Children might be placed in groups. The group that can suggest the greatest number of concepts (each including a minimum number of items, perhaps three or four) wins.

□ **For Sports-Minded Youngsters**. Ask students to listen to the radio, watch TV, or read the sports page of the newspaper to note the various terms that can be used to tell that one team defeated another, e.g.: UCLA *downed* Michigan 21-14, or they overthrew, upset, conquered, beat, whipped, triumphed over, routed, smashed, overwhelmed, toppled, put down, etc., the opponent. Or, the opposite type of description might be used: UCLA *bowed* to Michigan 14-21, or they were humbled by, yielded to, etc., the opponent. (For this activity the teacher should allude to the game of the season.)

After students have had time to prepare, the following activity might be engaged in: The teacher or a student sits facing the group of players. The leader has a bean bag, which he throws to a player. The player receiving the bean bag must immediately throw it back and simultaneously state a sentence of the prescribed type, e.g., Wisconsin *overwhelmed* Illinois 48-7, or Purdue *squeezed through* with a 14-13 victory. A term once used cannot be used again. The student scores a point for every acceptable response, and the student with the greatest number of points wins.

Teams may be used instead of individuals, if desired.

□ **Use Nonsense Words**. Compose three or more sentences. In each sentence use a common word, but each time with a different meaning. For the common word, substitute a nonsense word. Ask the children to write the real word, e.g.:

1. My bicycle is *jamper*.
2. The sun is almost *jamper*.
3. The moon is not *jamper*. It's white.
4. He's *jamper*. Yes, I've heard he's a coward.

jamper = _____

□ **Sight Vocabulary**. To help the child transfer words to his sight vocabulary, wide reading is most useful, especially if the child is allowed to read what he likes. Some children enjoy using flash cards, but when these are used without context, learning may be arid—or nil.

□ **Hand Tachistoscopes**. Hand tachistoscopes can be made in many shapes of interest to a child. In the tachistoscope, there is a rectangular slot. Inserted behind the slot is a long strip of rolled paper with words, or preferably phrases, typed or printed on it.

The words or phrases are exposed one at a time for a brief interval while the child reads them, or learns to read them, at sight. A bowling pin is a good form for a tachistoscope.

| was playing |
| was singing |
| was laughing |
| was jumping |
| was leaving |
| was going |
| was swimming |
| (etc.) |

| a boy |
| a girl |
| a bird |
| a robin |
| a wren |
| a duck |
| a sparrow |
| (etc.) |

Miscellaneous

Utilizing Morphology in Reading

A morpheme is the smallest unit of meaning in a language. There are two general types of morphemes in English, as in other languages. An uninflected word is a *free morpheme*. For example, the following are free English morphemes: cat, elephant, house, school, month. Units of language that have meaning but that cannot stand alone as words are *bound morphemes*. Prefixes, some roots, and suffixes are bound morphemes. For example, the following are bound morphemes: un-, re-, sub-, intra-; geo-, bio-, -logy, -nym; -ful, -ing, -ed.

In a reading program, it is common practice to sequence teaching from easy to difficult. It is easiest for children to understand compounding, especially when two free English morphemes are used. The following types of compound words might be used in the early stages of a program: milkman, mailman, oatmeal, outlaw.

As a next step, commonly used *bound* morphemes might be combined with *free* English morphemes. Some common prefixes thus used are: un-, in-, dis-, re-, sub-. Words introduced at this stage might be: unkind, unable, unafraid, unhappy; inactive, incorrect, inhuman, insecure; disagree, disappear, dislike, distrust; reappear, reopen, readjust, refill; subsoil, submarine, subway, subtropical.

From such combinations, children easily learn that when a prefix is added to a word they know, the meaning of the word is changed, or altered, by the meaning of the prefix. Thus *unkind* means not kind; *unable* means not able; *inactive* means

27

not active; *disagree* means the opposite of agree; *subsoil* means under the top soil.

Children also learn to add suffixes to *free* English morphemes. For example, they learn to add -s, -es, -ed, -ing to roots, thus: boy – boys; box – boxes; look – looked; go – going. These suffixes are inflectional in nature. Children also learn to add meaning endings such as -ful and -less: thoughtful, thoughtless; powerful, powerless.

Then they are ready for more difficult things, such as adding more difficult prefixes to *free* English morphemes: transcontinental, underpaid. Next they are taught to combine two *bound* morphemes: concede, extract, geology.

They learn that when words are composed of two or more morphemes, syllabic divisions almost always come between the morphemes:

prefix – root: co/operate, un/kind, ex/pand

root   – root: milk/man, oat/meal, pseudo/nym

root   – suffix: go/ing, noise/less, thought/ful

Of course, there might also be syllabication divisions *within* morphemes. In such cases, usually phonic syllabication generalizations describe where the division will come.

Following are some activities for teaching children about morphemes.

EASY COMPOUNDS

☐   **Pair-Off Pictures.** Cut out pictures from magazines which illustrate each root of a compound. Arrange the two pictures in order from left to right, putting a plus sign between them. Ask the child to say or write the compound, e.g.:

 +  = _____

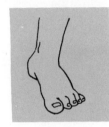 +  = _____

☐   **Sentence Completion.** Read sentences to children, or have them read the sentences. Children suggest the compound word which completes the sentence. For example:

1. A bird that is blue might be a_____.
2. A case for books is a _____.
3. A plane that can land on the sea is a _____.
4. A ball that you kick with your foot is a _____.
5. A bonnet to protect a lady from the sun is a

    _____.

6. A skin from a sheep is a_____.
7. Light from the moon is _____.
8. A field of corn is a _____.
9. A boat with sails is a_____.
10. A ball made of snow is a _____.

Write the compound words on the board. Ask the children to pronounce each word. Begin teaching the concept of syllabication by pointing out to the children that there is a brief break, or pause, between the two roots. Ask one child, then another, to come to the board to draw a slash between the two roots, thus:

blue/bird	book/case	sea/plane
foot/ball	sun/bonnet	sheep/skin
moon/light	corn/field	sail/boat
snow/ball		

☐ **Pair Off Roots.** List initial roots on the left side of the paper (or board) and final roots on the right side. Ask the children to combine them to make words. Ask them to use each word in a sentence—or to draw a picture of it.

Easy Compounds

Initial roots		*Final roots*	
boy	out	writer	ball
ice	type	house	boat
base	air	cream	friend
steam	light	port	field

☐ **Pair Off Children.** Using the following list, or another that you wish to make, count off half the number of words as you have children in your class. Using these words, write each root on a separate card.

oat/meal	sea/plane	life/boat	sun/shine
after/noon	hand/bag	cow/boy	mail/man
pea/cock	bed/room	rain/fall	neck/lace
grand/father	eye/brow	nest/egg	butter/fly

Pass out one card to each child. Then ask each child to find the other half of his compound. The two children draw a picture illustrating their word.

☐ **Five Teams.** Write fifty words, such as the following, on the board in five columns.

stick	knife	sun	rail	cream
shoe	oat	battle	sail	nut
sea	hook	lace	house	book

foot	broom	bird	jack	eye
man	road	cake	pecker	plane
skin	set	step	sheep	field
wood	paper	pea	brows	blue
grand	play	news	pan	fish
neck	post	mother	case	boat
ground	ice	meal	snow	wife

Form the class into five teams—or choose leaders, and have each leader select his or her team.

Each team is assigned one of the above columns. They write ten compound words, using each root in their column with another root from another column. The first team to have ten correct words wins.

The ten words are then written on the board, and members of the class suggest sentences using these words.

Variation. Duplicate copies of the above list, and ask each child to write 25 words using these roots. Have each child illustrate each word or use it in a sentence.

Easy
Compounds

EASY PREFIXES

☐   **Word Wheels.** In Thorndike's word list of the twenty-thousand most common words in English, there are five-thousand words that have prefixes. Eighty-two percent of these five-thousand words use one of the following prefixes:

ab – away from	*in* – into
ad – to, toward	*in* – not
be – on all sides, overly	*pre* – before
com, con, co – with, together	*pro* – in favor of, for, before
de – reversal, undoing, downward	*re* – again, restore
dis – not, reversal	*sub* – under, beneath
en – in, into, to cover	*un* – not
ex – out of, former	*un* – do the opposite of

Easy Prefixes

Each of these can be used in a word-wheel, using the prefix with free English morphemes when possible. For example:

sub = under, beneath

un = do the opposite of

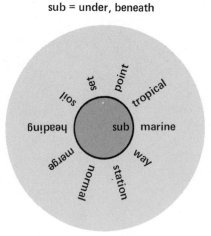
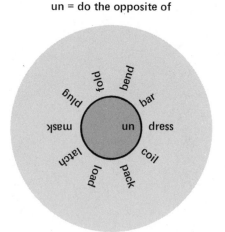

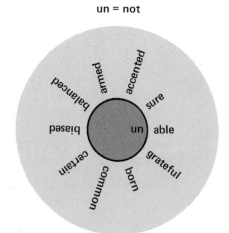

re = again, restore

un = not

Activity. Pair students off into teams. Turn word wheels upside down, and allow each team to draw one. Given a specified amount of time—five or ten minutes or possibly more—for team members to do the following:

1. *define* as many words as possible. These words are composed of the given prefix in combination with the given roots. (scoring: apiece - 1 point)

2. *use* in a meaningful sentence as many of these words as possible. (scoring: apiece - 1 point)

3. *write* additional words using the given prefix. (scoring: apiece - 2 points)

4. *define* as many of these words as possible. (scoring: apiece - 1 point)

5. *use* in a meaningful sentence as many of these words as possible. (scoring: apiece - 1 point)

The team with the greatest number of points wins.

☐   **Which Meaning?** Two of the prefixes listed in number 1, above, have two very different meanings. Write sentences with words in them that use these prefixes, and ask the children to tell which meaning the prefix has. For example:

in = not   or   in = into

**Easy
Prefixes**

1. The linoleum was *inlaid*.   in = <u>into</u>
2. The discussion was *informal*.   in = _____
3. Chicago is an *inland* city.   in = _____
4. We felt he was *insincere*.   in = _____
    Etc.

un = not   or   un = do the opposite of

1. His reputation was *unspotted*.   un = _____
2. We were *uncertain* of the result. un = _____
3. Dad had to *unpack*.   un = _____
4. I *untied* the package.   un = _____
    Etc.

☐   **Blocks.** Buy some wooden or foam rubber (for silence) cubes. Do them in sets thus: on one, print two to six different prefixes and on two or three others print roots, thus:

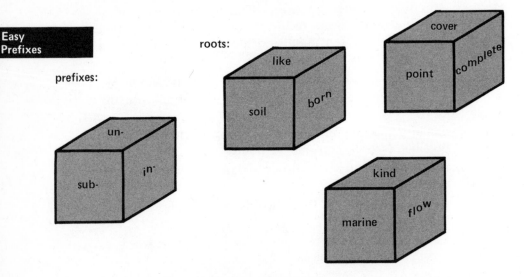

Easy
Prefixes

prefixes:

roots:

Have a set for every two children.

Pair the children off, and have them take turns tossing the blocks. They get one point each time they toss and come up with a word they can identify. It's possible to get two or three points on one toss. The child with the greatest number of points wins. The prefix cube might have the following on it:

sub, sub, in, in, un, un,

The root cubes might have the following on them:

cube 1	cube 2	cube 3
soil	marine	point
group	order	normal
road	laid	justice
born	flow	complete
like	kind	cover
tie	buckle	natural

☐ **Wordo.** List on the board about 30-35 free English or in-flected morphemes (root words) which could be combined with one of several specified prefixes or suffixes. Give each child a blank Wordo (Bingo) card, a form with 25 blank rectangles in a 5 × 5 position, with the middle rectangle marked FREE. Have each child select 24 of the morphemes and write each in one of the remaining rectangles.

Give children small pieces of tagboard with the specified prefixes or suffixes (several of each) on them. The teacher or a child reads a sentence using the root word and defining the prefix or suffix which goes with it. The player places the correct prefix or suffix over the root word on his card. Five horizontally, vertically, or diagonally wins—but check the winning card to be sure the child has done it correctly.

Additional root words which could be used with the following card are: united, even, grace, familiar, act, famous, forest, continue, obedient, experienced, popular, valid.

complete	elect	formal	cover	like
enter	visible	kind	pack	able
easy	accurate	FREE	fill	agree
active	honest	pleasant	write	afraid
appear	land	latch	happy	tied

in   dis   un   re

1. The story was *not complete* . . . not complete.
2. Henry said he would *not agree* with Peter . . . not agree.
3. Maria thought the picture was *not pleasant* . . . not pleasant.
4. The ghost suddenly was *not visible* . . . not visible.
5. The family was to be *united again* . . . united again.
    Etc.

☐   **Give an Example.**   Ask the children to supply examples for words with prefixes, e.g.:

1. One meaning of *in-* is *into.* Ask the children to give an example of something that is:

    inlaid   inbred   inland   intaken

2. Also, *-in* can mean *not.* Ask for an example of something that is:

    inaccurate   insincere   inhuman   inappropriate

3. The prefix *re-* often means *again.* Ask for an example of someone who was:

    reelected   reunited   reformed   remarried

4. The prefix *sub-* usually means *under.* Ask for an example of:

    a submarine   a subway   a subtropical region

5. *Co-* usually means with or together. Ask the children what it means if:

    two people *coexist.*

    two people are *copilots* or *coauthors.*

    a school is *coeducational.* What is a *co-ed?*

Easy
Prefixes

☐   **Syllabication.**   List prefixed words on the board. Ask the children to pronounce the words along with you. Have a piece of colored chalk available. Ask the children—one at a time—to underline a prefix and draw a slash to show where the word is divided into syllables. (Just divide between prefix and root—not within any morphemes.) E.g.:

un/fit   sub/marine   re/count   dis/appear

As they underline the prefix ask them to define it. Then ask them to define the word.

☐ **Highest Score Wins.** Within jets, balloons, and kites print selected morphemes. Allow the children a specific amount of time to write as many words as they can by combining these. The child who makes the highest score wins.

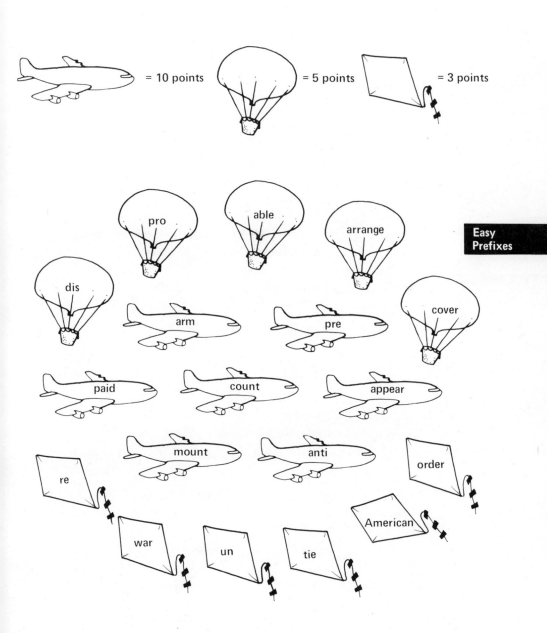

Easy
Prefixes

EASY SUFFIXES

☐ **Add an Ending.** List on a paper the following common inflectional endings:

-s   -ed   -ness   -ly
-es   -ing   -ment   -y

Write pairs of sentences, one of which requires the use of an ending listed above. Leave space for the child to write in the proper ending.

1. John loves to float in the water.
   John thinks float _____ is fun.
2. My dog is kind.
   Kind _____ is important in a dog.
3. Pedro walked up a step at a time.
   Then he took two step _____ at once.
4. Let us govern ourselves.
   Govern _____ by and for the people is a necessity.
5. José asked if he could look at the book.
   José look _____ , and he liked it.
6. Diane has a rowboat.
   Diane enjoys boat _____ .
7. Marcy enjoyed being like a mouse.
   Marcy was mous _____ .
8. On December 21, there was a box under the tree.
   On December 22, there were three box _____ there.
9. Gary was everyone's friend.
   Gary was friend _____ .
10. The road was slick with ice.
    Ic __ roads are slick.

☐ **Comparative Suffixes -er, -est.** Ask children to illustrate on paper—in sets—each of the following words. Or have them play charades, illustrating these in sets:

tall	dark	loud
taller	darker	louder
tallest	darkest	loudest

Easy Suffixes

proud	long	small
prouder	longer	smaller
proudest	longest	smallest

sad	good
sadder	better
saddest	best

☐ **Meaninfgul Suffixes -ful, -less.** Ask children to illustrate—or find pictures representing—each of the following pairs of words:

powerful	—	(e.g., a powerful person)
powerless	—	(e.g., a powerless person)

fearful	—	(e.g., a fearful elephant)
fearless	—	(e.g., a fearless mouse)

careful	—	(e.g., a careful Smokey the bear)
careless	—	(e.g., a careless traveler)

graceful	—	(e.g., a graceful diver)
graceless	—	(e.g., a graceless gooney bird)

Easy
Suffixes

☐ **Prefix or Suffix Interchange.** Divide the following words into syllables between the morphemes. Then combine the free morpheme or root with a bound morpheme from another word to make a new word.

uni/lateral	_bilateral_	thoughtful	_____
dislike	_____	monogamy	_____
polytheism	_____	bicycle	_____
asocial	_____	powerless	_____
unable	_____	antipathy	_____

☐ **Highest Score Wins.** Within jets, balloons, and kites print selected morphemes. Allow the children a specified amount of time to write as many words as they can by combining these. The child who makes the highest score wins.

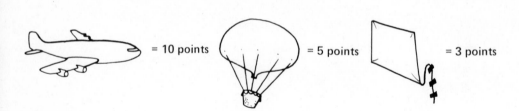

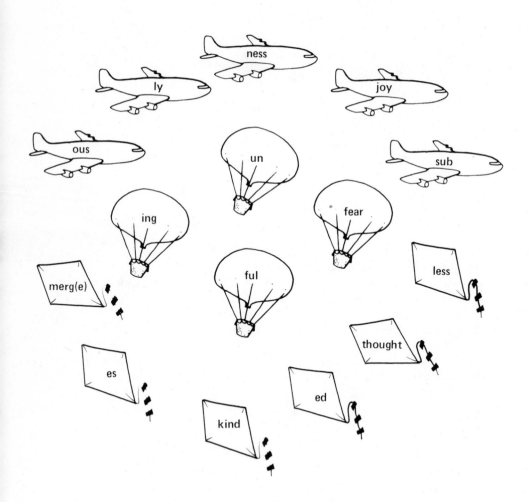

INTERESTING THEMES IN MORPHOLOGY

☐ **Number Morphemes.** Number morphemes are both interesting and useful. Included here are some of the most common ones.

English	Latin	Greek
one	uni	mono
two	bi, duo	di
three	tri	tri
four	quad, quar	
five	quin	
six	sex, sexi	hex, hexa
seven	sept	
eight	octa, octo, oct	
nine	nov	
ten	deci	dec, deca, deka
hundred	cent	
thousand	mil, mill	
many	multi	poly
half	semi, hemi	hemi
all	omni	pan

Themes

Prepare an exercise, such as the following. Have children fill in the blanks.

1. In the old Roman calendar, September was the _____th month of the year; October was the _____th month; November was the _____th month, and December was the _____th month.

2. How many people sing in a duet? _____ in a quartet? _____

3. How many angles does a triangle have? _____ an octagon? _____ a quadrangle? _____ a hexagon? _____

4. If *lith* means stone, what is a monolith? _____

_____

5. If *lateral* means side, what is a trilateral agreement? _____ a bilateral agreement? _____

6. How many wheels does a unicycle have?_____

7. What is a bipartisan foreign policy?_____

8. How long is a decade?_____ a millennium? _____ a century? _____

9. Is the American flag tricolored?_____

10. How many feet does a tripod have? _____ Are you a biped? _____ Name a quadruped._____ How many feet, or tentacles, does an octopus have? _____ What's a centipede? _____

11. What is a quadroon?_____ an octo - roon?_____

12. If *the*, or *theo*, means god, what is a polytheist?_____ _____ a monotheist?_____ _____

13. If *gamy* means marriage, what is a bigamist?_____ _____ a monogamist?_____ a polygamist?_____

14. What is a quintuplet?_____a triplet? _____ a quadruplet ? _____

Themes

15. What does it mean if someone has multitudinous ideas? _____

16. What is a semicircle?_____a hemisphere? _____

17. If we meet semiannually, how often do we meet?_____ _____ How often do we meet if we meet biannually? _____

18. What countries are in PanAmerica?_____

☐   **Dice Game.** From two to six children may play this game. Each child plays for himself if 2, 3, or 5 play. If 4 or 6 play, there should be two teams.

Use two dice. Children take turns—in clockwise order— tossing the dice. At one toss, a child can make 0, 1, 2, or 3 points for himself or for his team, thus:

1 point for giving a word using a bound morpheme for the number of dots on one die

1 point for giving a word using a bound morpheme for the number of dots on the other die

1 point for giving a word using a bound morpheme for the total number of dots on the two dice. Since total point value could be 11 or 12, for these use:

> *for 11*: cent or mil, or else semi or hemi
>
> *for 12*: poly or multi, or else pan or omni

A word that has been given once during the game cannot count again.

☐ **The Earth and Heavens.** Morphemes that have to do with the earth and the heavens are usually fascinating to children. Among the commonly used ones are:

stella ⎫		*sol* — sun	
astro ⎬ star		*luna* — moon	

cosmo ⎫	world or universe	*geo* ⎫	earth
cosm ⎬		*terra* ⎬	

Prepare an exercise, such as the following. Have children fill in the blanks.

Themes

1. If *-oid* means *like*, as in *manlike*, would you expect a starfish to be a member of the Aster*oid*ea class or the Sol*oid*ea class? _____
Why? _____

2. *Naut* means *navigator*, or *sailor*. Americans call theirs *astronauts* and Russians call theirs *cosmonauts*. Are both names appropriate? Why?_____

3. Is the earth in *solar* or *lunar* orbit? _____

4. Have our astronauts ever been in *solar* orbit?_____
in *lunar* orbit? _____

5. People once thought a person became a *lunatic*, or insane, because that person stared too long at the_____
_____.

6. What does *celestial* mean if it means the opposite of *terrestrial*?_____

7. *Polis* means city. Do you think Paris is a cosmo*poli*tan city? _____ Why? _____
   What do you think a *cosmopolite* is? _____

8. What is a dis*aster*? _____

9. "His success was *astro*nomical." What does *astro*nomical mean? _____
   Name someone you would consider to be a *stellar* success.
   _____

10. Saturn is encircled by rings composed of many small solid bodies. These bodies keep the sun from clearly entering its atmosphere. People are sometimes called *saturnine*. What do you think this means?_____
    _____

☐ **The Morpheme a-:** The prefix *a-* means not or without. Thus, if typical means usual, atypical means unusual, or not usual. Have students circle the correct word as suggested by context:

1. For some time Thoreau enjoyed the life of a hermit. At that time you might say he was_____.

   social   asocial   antisocial

2. Some people just don't seem to know what is right and what is wrong. They're not really moral, nor are they__
   _____ .

   immoral   amoral

   You might call them_____ .

   immoral   amoral

3. Herman's father insists that there is no God. You might call him a(n)_____.

   atheist   theist

Other words which could be used are: asexual, atrophy, asymmetrical, atonal, agnostic, aseptic.

☐ **Morpheme Tree.** A list of very common Greek and Latin roots is given on p. 47. Pick one at a time and have the class make a bulletin board tree. Written on each leaf or piece of fruit would be a word using that root. Another possibility is to use one morpheme for a whole tree (see Example A), or one for a branch (see Example B).

Themes

Example A

Example B

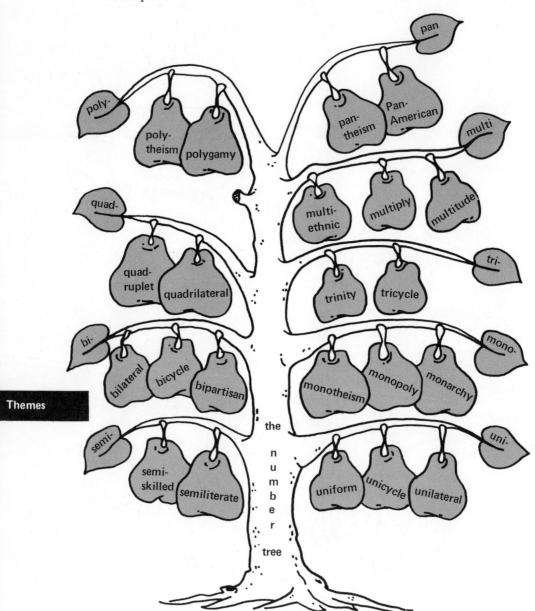

Themes

Greek

bio – life	micro – small	tele – far
geo – earth	scope – view	phon – sound
chrono – time	graph – write	theo – god
thermo – heat	auto – self	logy – science of, study of

Latin

duc, duct — to lead	scrib, script — to write
mit(t), miss — to send	tract — to pull
pend — to hang	cap — head
spec(t), spic — to look	card — heart
vid, vis — to see	man — hand
dic(t) — to say	

Example B

Using number morphemes, make a number tree. Give each child paper of the appropriate color for the fruit to be used and have him cut out several pieces of fruit. Then have him write a word on each piece, using one of the bound morphemes which represents a number. Then have the child hang his fruit on the appropriate branch of the tree.

☐ **Blends.** In English we sometimes take *part* of one morpheme and combine it with *part* of another to make a new word. For example, we have taken the first part of *smoke* and combined it with the last part of *fog* to get *smog*. Ask children to suggest other blends, for example:

*br*eak*fast* + *lunch* =		*tw*ist + wh*irl* =	
*mo*t*or* + ho*tel* =		*beef* + buff*alo* =	
*bo*at + ho*tel* =		*sk*irt + sh*ort* =	
*sl*ip + gl*ide* =		*fl*oat + ho*tel* =	

Children might enjoy making up some of their own.

☐ **Acronyms.** In English we sometimes take just the first letters in a series of morphemes or words to make a new word. For example, SNAFU is taken from "situation *n*ormal — *a*ll *f*ouled *u*p." Ask children for other examples. Also ask children to make up some of their own.

Examples

UNESCO	SALT	RADAR
CARE	WAVES	SONAR

☐   **Acronym Search.**

P	I	V	O	T	N	S	S	I	M	E	W
U	P	L	D	E	U	B	A	L	D	A	Z
N	A	T	O	Z	C	M	C	R	C	I	Y
A	P	D	N	O	N	F	W	S	P	Z	K
S	B	A	G	E	S	D	Y	I	W	J	B
U	P	R	A	D	A	R	X	K	U	E	Z
G	F	H	P	O	L	C	N	S	A	L	N
U	V	G	T	R	T	A	S	D	J	H	M
F	D	S	A	E	X	R	W	A	V	E	S
A	R	N	T	W	R	Y	I	I	O	M	N
N	O	F	R	I	V	A	S	S	D	G	O
S	U	Q	E	O	W	D	C	K	U	F	O
E	O	C	S	E	N	U	J	M	N	C	B
Y	M	C	A	M	O	B	X	O	P	I	D
A	E	N	C	A	B	U	C	S	U	S	K

Themes

Write the acronym in the blank following the words it represents. Then ring the acronym in the chart above. An acronym may read vertically, horizontally, or diagonally in any direction.

1. Situation Normal—All Fouled Up   SNAFU

2. North Atlantic Treaty Organization   _____

3. Strategic Arms Limitations Talks   _____

4. Australia, New Zealand, United States (Treaty)   _____

5. United Nations Education, Scientific, and Cultural Organization   _____

6. North, East, West, South   _____

7. Women's Army Corps   _____

8. Women Accepted for Volunteer Emergency Service (Navy)   _____

9. Cooperative for American Remittances Everywhere   _____

10. SOund NAvigation Ranging   _____

11. RAdio Detecting And Ranging   _____

12. Unidentified Flying Object   _____

13. Self-Contained Underwater Breathing Apparatus   _____

14. Very Important Person   _____

15. Young Men's Christian Assocation   _____

16. Young Women's Christian Association   _____

17. United States of America   _____

18. Union of Socialistic Soviet Republics   _____

☐   **Consonant Shift and Morpheme Cognates.** Grimm's Law (named after one of the brothers Grimm of fairytale fame, who first discovered what happened) describes the very regular consonant shift which occurred in the language which is the ancestor of English. Simply, this is what happened:

bh → b → p → f

dh → d → t → th

gh → g → k → h

Thus *pater* became *father*,
and *gno* became *know*.

Later we borrowed related words from other languages, and we frequently use these in rather formal situations. For example, we borrowed *pater* from Latin and the root *gno* from Greek. We use *father* and *fatherly* in everyday familiar English, but we use *paternal* in more formal situations and with a somewhat different meaning. Also, we use *know* very commonly, but dia*gno*se and a*gno*stic are more formal.

Below are other examples:

Grimm's Law describes these sound (and spelling) shifts:

From named language we later borrowed a cognate and used it in the following words:

Original	New	Language	Words
dent	tooth, teeth	Latin	*dent*al, *dent*ist, in*dent*
gno	know	Greek	dia*gno*se, a*gno*stic
pater	father	Latin	*pater*nal
mater	mother	Latin	*mater*nal
ped	foot, feet	Latin	*ped*al, *ped*estal, tri*pod*
centum	hundred	Latin	*cent*, *cent*ipede
pisces	fish	Latin	*pisc*ary, *Pisce*s
kardiakos	heart	GK and L	*cardiac*
canis	hound	GK and L	*canine*
corn	horn	Latin	*corn*ucopia
tris	three	GK and L	*tri*-(*tri*angle, *tri*cycle, etc.)
host	guest	Latin	*host*

Themes

Content of a Phonics Program

Phonics is an essential component of every word attack program. **Chapter 3**
And, in English, there are really not very many phonic principles
for children to learn—somewhere between twelve and twenty,
depending upon how they are counted. In this chapter, the
basic, necessary, and probably *only* phonic generalizations that
should be taught are given. Each is followed by English words
which exemplify the generalization.

Chapter 4 contains a discussion of and suggested activities
for teaching these generalizations in an elementary school
program. The discussion is brief, and it is suggested that the
reader study a modern commercial program—or better still,
compare several—to see the variety of techniques which are used
to teach these generalizations.[1] The suggested activities in
Chapter 4 should prove to be valuable for supplementary work
in a classroom.

Starred (★) generalizations in the present chapter are those
which the author has found many middle-grade and high-school
students need help in understanding and using.[2] Methodology

[1] See Appendixes D and E for a list of such programs and for common
sequential patterns used to teach phonics in developmental programs.

[2] Lou E. Burmeister, "An Analysis of the Inductive and Deductive Group
Approaches for Teaching Selected Word-Analysis Generalizations to
Disabled Readers in the Secondary School." Unpublished Doctoral
Dissertation, The University of Wisconsin, 1966. Also see Lou E.
Burmeister, "Selected Word Analysis Generalizations for a Group Approach
to Corrective Reading in the Secondary School," *Reading Research Quarterly* **IV** (Fall 1968): 71-95.

for teaching these in a mature way is sometimes included directly after these generalizations in the present chapter. Since several research studies have indicated that college students and teachers themselves often do not know these generalizations,[3] it is suggested that the reader of this book may wish to work these exercises as he goes along so that he, himself, will better understand and be able to enunciate the content of a phonics program.

To understand the discussion, it is essential that the reader be familiar with the following terminology:

Phoneme: *phon*= sound, *eme*= smallest unit
  A phoneme is the smallest unit of sound.

The word *cat* has three phonemes.	/k/+/ă/+/t/
The word *man* has three phonemes .	/m/+/ă/+/n/
The word *main* has three phonemes.	/m/+/ā/+/n/
The word *potato* has six phonemes.	/p/+/ə/+/t/+/ā/+/t/+/ō/

Grapheme: *graph*= writing, written symbol, *eme*= smallest unit
  A grapheme is a written symbol for the phoneme it represents.

The word *cat* has three graphemes.	c + a + t
The word *man* has three graphemes.	m + a + n

---

[3] See Ira E. Aaron, "What Teachers and Prospective Teachers Know about Phonic Generalizations," *Journal of Educational Research* 53 (May 1960): 323-330. Also George D. Spache and Mary E. Baggett, "What Do Teachers Know about Phonics and Syllabication?" *The Reading Teacher* 19 (November 1965): 96-99. Also James T. Fleming, "Teachers' Understanding of Phonic Generalizations." *The Reading Teacher* 25 (January 1972): 400-404. And Mary C. Austin, *The Torch Lighters*, Cambridge, Mass.: Harvard University Press, 1961, pp. 46-47.

A few linguists and educators have argued that since many teachers do not know phonic generalizations, and since teachers presumably can read, the teaching of phonics is unnecessary. On the surface, this argument may appear to be logical.

However, there is a vast difference between being able to state a generalization, or even being able to identify it in writing, and consciously or subconsciously being able to apply it.

Many people apply generalizations who could never state them; the opposite is also true. Children—and readers in general—need not be able to *state* phonic generalizations. However, in order to directly *teach* phonic generalizations, *teachers* do have to be consciously aware of these generalizations.

The word *main* has three graphemes.   m + ai + n

The word *mane* has three graphemes.   m + a_e + n

The word *Maine* has three graphemes.   M + ai_e + n

Digraph: *di*= two, *graph*= written symbol

A digraph is composed of two adjacent letters which represent one phoneme.

The following are consonant digraphs: th, sh, ph, ch, ng (*th*ink, *th*at, *sh*ould, *ph*oto, *ch*icken, si*ng*)

In this chapter particularly useful grapheme to phoneme relationships are discussed in the following order:

I.   Consonants

    A.   Single consonants

        1.   Consistent consonants

        2.   The consonants *c* and *g*

        3.   The consonants *q* and *s* and *x*

    B.   Double consonants (and consonant clusters)

        1.   Consonant blends

        2.   Consonant digraphs

        3.   Silent consonants

II.   Vowels

    A.   Definitions

    B.   Single vowel graphemes

        1.   Closed syllable

        2.   Open syllable

        3.   Final *y*

    C.   Final vowel-consonant-e

        1.   General rule

        2.   Exceptions

    D.   Vowel pairs

        1.   First vowel long, second vowel silent

        2.   Diphthongs

        3.   Broad *a* (circumflex *o*)

        4.   Long and short *oo*

        5.   The vowel pairs *ei* and *ie*

    E.   The consonantizing of *i*

III. Phonic syllabication
    A. Determination of a syllable
    B. Syllabication generalizations
        1. Situation: vowel-consonant-consonant-vowel
        2. Situation: vowel-consonant-vowel
        3. Situation: final consonant-l-e

PART I

Particularly Useful Grapheme to Phoneme Relationships

    Consonants
    A. Single Consonants
    B. Double Consonants (and Consonant Clusters)

SINGLE CONSONANTS — CONSISTENT CONSONANTS

Each consonant (except c, g, q, s, and x) is highly consistent in representing one sound:

b		d		f	
bat	hub	dog	bed	farm	elf
ball	cob	doll	food	face	leaf
bounce	tab	dug	glad	foot	roof
bird	web	dive	toad	fire	beef
bunny	jab	dirt	red	fudge	loaf

h^4		j^4		k	
house		jay		king	silk
hat		jet		kick	steak
head		juice		kind	wink
hawk		joy		kiss	park
honey		jeep		kite	week

l		m		n	
love	pail	man	dim	name	corn
lace	deal	map	gum	near	down
long	girl	monkey	swim	new	coon
lady	heal	male	farm	nut	fan
leaf	jail	milk	jam	navy	gun

p		r		t	
ping	cap	rat	jar	table	hat
pong	chip	rabbit	bear	tick	coat
palm	carp	rent	fur	tock	cat
party	jeep	reef	door	tug	eat
pine	nap	rib	your	town	bat

---

[4] The consonants h and j are not found in the final position.

**Single
Consonants—
Consistent**

v	
view	lov(e)
vase	wav(e)
voice	div(e)
vote	hiv(e)
very	liv(e)

w^5
wasp
would
wig
week
west

y^5
yellow
yet
yes
yawn
yard

z	
zebra	froz(e)
zoo	priz(e)
zone	haz(e)
zero	doz(e)
zest	whiz

---

[5] w and y are not found *as consonants* in the final position. They do serve in the final position as vowels, however: cow, snow; by, my, pay, etc.

★ SINGLE CONSONANTS — c AND g

When c or g is followed by e, i, or y, it represents its soft sound. When followed by anything else, or nothing, it represents its hard sound. Omit ch and gh.

c-soft	c-hard	g-soft	g-hard
city	attic	gem	game
certain	cram	agile	goat
cycle	clash	gym	flag
dance	scar	engine	wagon
face	arc	orange	wig

Methodology for teaching students in the middle grades and above follows.

☐ **Teach the Following Generalization Inductively.** When c is followed by e i, or y, it represents an s *sound*; otherwise it represents a k *sound* (i.e., when followed by a, o, u, a consonant, or when it's the last letter in a word). Omit ch.

1. Ask students to give you a few words that have c's in them.

    a) Write them on the board. For example:

    cat   cake   cyclone   accelerate

    b) Underline the c's, and say the words (visual and auditory discrimination).

    c) Ask students if they hear two different sounds (auditory discrimination).

    d) Ask students what two different letters are often used to spell these sounds (s, k).

2. Ask students to draw two wide columns on a piece of paper. In the first column have them write ten words that have c's in them that represent the s *sound*. In the second column they should write ten words that have c's in them that represent the k *sound*. Encourage students to use a textbook or newspaper to locate the words. Any word that has a c in it will fit in one column or the other (except ch).

c

c = /s/	c = /k/
1. *c*ity – i	1. atti*c* – _
2. *c*ycle – y	2. re*c*oup – o
3. *c*ertain – e	3. ac*c*ept – c
4. ni*c*e – e	4. *c*antelope – a
•	•
•	•
•	•
10.	10.

c and g

Next, have students write the letter that follows each *c*.

3. Ask the class what letters follow the *c*'s when the *c*'s represent the *s sound*. They should respond *e, i,* or *y.* If anyone responds with another letter, he has probably made a mistake, having put the word in the wrong column. (Exceptions are very rare!) Ask if anyone has an *e, i,* or *y* following the *c* when the *c* represents the *k sound.* Ask the students to formulate the generalization.

4. Give them the following exercise:

Write an *s* after the following words if the *c* represents an *s* sound; write a *k* if it represents a *k* sound.

1. *c*ity	_____	13. dynami*c*	___,___
2. *c*ider	_____	14. a*cc*elerate	___,___
3. *c*ake	_____	15. obstru*c*t	_____
4. *c*asual	_____	16. o*c*tet	_____
5. *c*y*c*le	___,___	17. va*c*illate	_____
6. atti*c*	_____	18. *c*ar*c*inoma	___,___
7. re*c*itative	_____	19. skepti*c*	_____
8. do*c*ile	_____	20. skepti*c*ism	_____
9. re*c*on*c*ile	___,___	21. vi*c*e	_____
10. a*cc*ount	___,___	22. su*cc*ess	___,___
11. re*c*oup	_____	23. su*cc*in*c*t	___,___,___
12. fa*c*titious	_____	24. ta*c*t	_____

How will knowing this rule help you? _____

_____

_____

Have students pronounce these words and use them in sentences.

☐ **Teach the Following Generalization Inductively.** Usually when *g* is followed by *e, i,* or *y,* it represents a *j sound* (soft); otherwise it represents the *hard g sound,* as in go. Omit *gh.*

1. Ask students to give you a few words that have *g*'s in them.

   a) Write them on the board. For example:

      *g*ift   *g*ot   *g*ym   su*gg*est

      (At this point don't worry if the words do not follow the generalization. About 10% of our words do not. Anglo-Saxon words—the simplest words in our language—are the common exceptions. By second or third grade most students already have these words in their sight vocabularies. They need not use phonics on such words, e.g., give, get, girl, tiger, finger, forget, forgive).

   b) Underline the *g*'s, and say the words (visual and auditory discrimination).

   c) Ask the students if they hear two different sounds (auditory discrimination).

   d) Ask students what letter is frequently used to spell the soft sound (*j*).

2. Ask students to draw two wide columns on a piece of paper. In the first column have them write ten words that have *g*'s in them that represent the *j sound*. In the second column they should write ten words that have *g*'s in them that represent the *hard g sound*. Encourage students to use a textbook or newspaper to locate the words. Any word that has a *g* in it will fit in one column or the other (except *gh* and many *gn* words).

g

g = /j/			*g* as in go		
1. gesture	–	e	1. girl	–	i
2. strange	–	e	2. globe	–	l
3. gypsy	–	y	3. flag	–	–
4. frigid	–	i	4. gas	–	a
•			•		
•			•		
•			•		
10.			10.		

Next have the student write the letter that follows each *g*.

3. Ask the class what letters follow the *g*'s when the *g*'s represent the *j sound*. They should respond *e*, *i*, or *y*. If anyone responds with another letter, he has probably made a mistake, having put the word in the wrong column.

   Ask what letters follow the *g* when it represents a hard sound. Usually anything but *e*, *i*, or *y*, although there will be some exceptions. Write the exceptions on the board, and point out that most of these words are Anglo-Saxon words—easy words—which they know by sight. Ask the students to formulate the generalization.

4. Give them the following exercise.

   Write a *j* after the following words if the *g* represents a *j sound*; write a *g* if it represents the *g sound*, as in *go*.

1. suggest	_____,_____	8. malignant	_____
2. pugilist	_____	9. gift	_____
3. gas	_____	10. greedy	_____
4. garnish	_____	11. indigent	_____
5. flag	_____	12. indignant	_____
6. gesticulation	_____	13. frigid	_____
7. congress	_____	14. contiguous	_____

15. tiger   _____   20. impregnable _____
16. vague   _____   21. segregate   _____,_____
17. globe   _____   22. incongruent _____
18. misogamy   _____   23. gregarious   _____,_____
19. misogyny   _____   24. gypsy   _____

How will knowing this rule help you?

_____

Have students pronounce these words and use them in sentences.

c and *g*

SINGLE CONSONANTS — *q* AND *s* AND *x*

Several consonants are slightly inconsistent in the sounds they represent. These consonants are:

1. *The Letter* **Q**. The letter *q*, always followed by *u*, represents the following sounds: /kw/ as in queen and request (91% of the time), and /k/ as in bouquet (6% of the time).

q, s, x

   qu = /kw/

queen	aquatic	require	quail	quilt
quest	equip	quit	quake	frequent
quick	inquire	quote	qualify	quadrant
quill	quiet	quack	quart	request

2. *The Letter* **S**. The letter *s* usually (86% of the time) represents its own sound (swim, soft, solo). Its next most frequent sound (/z/ - 11%) is found in words such as resort, raisin, music, desire, treason. Omit *sh*.

s = /s/		*s* = /z/	
sun	gas	daisy	busy
silent	bus	music	easy
sea	mouse	reason	closet
silk	bumps	season	cruise
silver	horse	weasel	arose

3. *The Letter* **X**. The letter *x* represents the sounds found in the following words (/ks/ or /k/ - /s/): ax, box, tax; foxy, taxi, vixen, and (/g/ - /z/): exact, exempt, exist, example.

x = /ks/		*x* = /k/- /s/[6]	*x* = /g/- /z/[6]
fix	excuse	axis	exhibit
fox	explore	proxy	exalt
ox	expert	toxic	exert
mix	expand	oxygen	executive
six	exchange	galaxy	exam

---

[6] I.e., syllabic division falls between /k/ and /s/ or between /g/ and /z/.

DOUBLE CONSONANTS (AND TRIPLE CONSONANTS) — BLENDS

When two unlike consonants appear side-by-side, usually the sound represented is a blend of the sounds represented by each (*bl*ock, *dr*own, *gr*ow, *sm*ile, *sp*ook, *spl*ash, etc.)

In English there are common blend "families." These are given below.

1. *L Family:* _____l

bl-	*cl-*	*fl-*	*gl-*	*pl-*	*sl-*
blue	clown	flag	glass	please	sleep
block	cling	flea	glow	plank	slick
blast	class	flirt	glint	plow	slot
blind	clump	flow	glad	plead	slap
blame	clear	flap	glare	plump	slump
blood	clash	flock	gleam	plane	slim

2. *R Family:* _____r

br-	*cr-*	*dr-*	*fr-*	*gr-*	*pr-*
brown	crab	drive	free	green	prune
brain	cream	dream	frame	grave	pray
break	crime	drain	frill	grim	preach
brick	crowd	drop	fresh	group	prick
broth	crush	drift	frog	greet	prod
breathe	crate	drum	frost	groove	proud

tr-	*str-*	*thr-*
tree	stream	throw
trail	stretch	three
troop	street	thread
trench	strain	thrill
trick	streak	throat
trout	strange	throne

3. *S Family*:   s____

sc-	*sk-/-sk*	*sl-*	*sm-*	*sn-*
scold	skunk	slow	smile	snow
scarf	skit	sleet	smooth	snake
scowl	skull	slam	smack	sniff
scale	dusk	slink	smell	snug
scope	risk	slope	smash	snore
scare	brisk	slug	smog	snail

sp-/-sp	*st-/-st*	*sw-*	*sch-*	*scr-*
spat	stamp	swim	school	scrape
spare	stick	swamp	scheme	scream
spin	steal	swell	schooner	screech
clasp	quest	swish	schedule	scroll
wasp	pest	swipe	scholar	scratch
crisp	test	sweep	schizoid	screen

spl-	*spr-*	*str-*
splash	spring	strip
splotch	sprig	street
splendid	sprain	stripe
splinter	sprout	stroll
split	spread	strap
splurge	spray	strum

4. *T Family:* ____t

-ft	*-lt*	*-nt*	*-st*
raft	halt	dent	mist
lift	guilt	grant	crust
soft	salt	sprint	cost
left	spilt	lint	trust
sift	wilt	print	frost
drift	belt	went	pest

Double Consonants— Blends

5. *D Family:* _____d

-ld	*-nd*
scold	spend
build	grand
bold	fund
held	brand
fold	blond
mold	stand

6. *P Family:* _____p

-mp	*-sp*
stamp	clasp
lump	lisp
plump	wasp
champ	grasp
stump	crisp
cramp	gasp

Double Consonants— Blends

DOUBLE CONSONANTS — DIGRAPHS

Although spelled with two consonants, consonant digraphs function as single consonants. The digraphs in English are *ch*, *sh*, *th*, *ph*, *ng*, and possibly *ck*. The most common sounds each represents are given below.

1. *ch* represents three sounds:

    /ch/ as in child, chop 63%
    /k/ as in chorus, christen, orchid 30%
    /sh/ as in chef, chute, mustache 7%

2. *sh* represents /sh/ as in should, ship, shed.

3. *th* represents two sounds:

    / ð / as in this, they, rhythm (voiced) 74%
    / θ / as in think, thick, youth (voiceless) 26%

4. *ph* represents /f/ as in elephant, photo.

5. *ng* represents / ŋ / as in sing, wing, young.

6. *ck* represents /k/ as in chick, package, cuckoo.

    (ck is really not a digraph, but is rather two like consonants together, in which c represents /k/ and is silent. See next section.)

Examples

ch = /ch/		*ch* = /k/	*ch* = /sh/
chocolate	chose	character	chute
chow	chicken	chorus	chef
champion	chief	chronic	machine
chant	chill	chord	chandelier
chore	choose	chrome	parachute

sh = /sh/	
should	shed
ship	shop
push	thrush

th = / ð /		*th* = / θ /	
rhythm	mother	think	throw
there	leather	thief	thumb
this	either	thirsty	thump
father	weather	thorn	thirteen

ph = /f/

elephant	alphabet
photo	phrase
typhoon	phone
dolphin	gopher

ng = / ŋ /

ring	young
gong	long
string	sting
wing	song

Double
Consonants—
Digraphs

DOUBLE CONSONANTS — SILENT CONSONANTS

Sometimes when two consonants appear side by side, one is silent. For example:

1. When two *like* consonants are side-by-side, they represent only one sound. (This is not true of *cc* or *gg* when followed by *e, i,* or *y*—suc*cess*, sug*gest*.) Examples are egg, guppy, guerilla, tattoo. Also:

bb =	/b/:	ebb, robber, bubble, cobbler, lobby
cc =	/k/:	accuse, moccasin, yucca, raccoon, occur (but *cc* = /k/-/s/: succinct, accelerate, accent)
ck =	/k/:	brick, pocket, locker, rocky, check, jack
dd =	/d/:	odd, add, daddy, saddle, paddle, sudden
ff =	/f/:	off, stuff, coffee, giraffe, office, differ
gg =	/g/:	egg, beggar, foggy, giggle, wiggle, toboggan (but *gg* = /g/-/j/: suggest - rare, no other examples)
ll =	/l/:	ball, llama, hello, collide, bullet
mm =	/m/:	hammock, dummy, summer, mummy, common
nn =	/n/:	inn, annoy, bunny, sunny, tennis, penny
pp =	/p/:	puppy, happy, dipper, pepper, puppet
rr =	/r/:	horrid, marry, corral, arrow, cherry
ss =	/s/:	boss, class, blossom, gossip, assign
tt =	/t/:	mitt, tattoo, cotton, bottle, clutter, kettle

   Silent Consonants

2. When certain *unlike* consonants are side-by-side in the same syllable, only one sound is represented. This is true of the following pairs: *initial kn-*, as in kneel, knot; *initial ps-*, as in psalm, pseudo; *initial wr-*, as in wrap, write; *final -dg (e)*, as in dodge, bridge; *final -gn*, as in sign, reign, but also *initial gn-*, as in gnat, gnome; *final -lm*, as in calm, palm; *final -mb*, as in bomb, comb; *final -tch*, as in catch, witch.[7]

---

[7]See Appendix A.

kn- = /n/

knowledge	knee	knew	knob	knat
knack	knell	knight	knock	know
knave	knelt	knit	knoll	knife
knead				

ps- = /s/

psalm	psaltery	pseudo	psyche	psychic

wr- = /r/

write	wrath	wrung	wrest	wrist
wrap	wreak	wreck	wretch	writhe
wrack	wreathe	wren	wring	wroth
wraith	write	wrench	wrinkle	wry
wrangle	wrong			

-dg(e) = /j/

badge	lodge	fledge	ledge	ridge
badger	dodge	fledgling	ledger	sedge
grudge	dredge	fudge	lodge	sledge
bridge	drudge	gadget	midget	smudge
budget	edge	hedge	nudge	stodgy
cudgel	fidget	judge	pledge	wedge
knowledge	partridge			

Silent Consonants

gn-/-gn = /n/

gnash	align	cologne	feign	sign
gnat	assign	consign	impugn	ensign
gnaw	benign	design	malign	foreign
gnu	champaign	deign	reign	sovereign

-lm = /m/

almond	psalm	salmon	calm
alms	qualm	palm	balm

-mb = /m/

aplomb	comb	lamb	plumber	thumb
bomb	dumb	limb	succumb	tomb
climb	jamb	numb		

-tch = /ch/

batch	etch	ketch	pitcher	stretch
blotch	fetch	kitchen	satchel	switch
butcher	hatch	latch	scotch	thatch
catch	hatchet	match	scratch	twitch
clutch	hitch	notch	sketch	watch
crotch	hutch	patch	snatch	witch
crutch	itch	pitch	stitch	wretch
ditch				

**Silent
Consonants**

PART II

Particularly Useful Grapheme to Phoneme Relationships

Vowels

A. Definitions

B. Single Vowel Graphemes

C. Final Vowel - Consonant - E

D. Vowel Pairs

E. Consonantizing of *i*

VOWELS—DEFINITIONS

The five vowels (*a,e,i,o,u*) and two "semivowels" (*y* and *w*) are used singly and in pairs and in the final vowel (consonant) *-e* position to represent a variety of sounds. The most common sounds are the vowel's own short sound (h*a*t, p*e*t, h*i*t, h*o*t, h*u*t); the long sound (m*ai*n, m*ea*t, s*i*ze, *oa*k, c*u*te); a schwa (*a*bout, cam*e*l, penc*i*l, lem*o*n, circ*u*s, marri*a*ge); and *r* modified sound (c*a*r, c*a*re, h*e*r, h*ea*r, f*o*r); a diphthong (*ou*t, c*ow*, c*oi*n, b*oy*); a *broad a*—or *circumflex o*—(*au*to, *aw*ful, b*a*ll), a long and short double *o* (r*oo*ster, b*oo*k).

The following charts are designed to supply examples of the most common vowel sounds in American English. Although common spellings for these sounds are used in the chart, it should be understood that other spellings are sometimes used to represent the same sounds. It should also be understood that there are sometimes dialectal variations in the phonemes that certain vowel graphemes represent.

Sound	Vowel				
	a	*e*	*i*	*o*	*u*
schwa: /ə/	*a*bout	par*e*nt	penc*i*l	lem*o*n	circ*u*s
short vowel: /v̆/	h*a*t	p*e*t	h*i*d	h*o*p	c*u*t
vowel modified by an *r*	c*a*r c*a*re	h*e*r h*e*re	f*i*r f*i*re	f*o*r f*o*re	h*u*rt c*u*re
long vowel: /v̄/	h*a*te	P*e*te	h*i*de	h*o*pe	c*u*te

Other sounds		Common spellings
diphthongs:	/oi/	c*oi*n, b*oy*
	/ou/	*ou*t, c*ow*
broad *a*:	/ô/	*au*to, *aw*ful, b*a*ll
also:	/ō͞o/	r*oo*ster, lag*oo*n
	/o͝o/	b*oo*k, c*oo*ky

Activity for students in the middle grades or above follows.

☐ **Spelling of Vowel Phonemes.** To show that vowel phonemes can be spelled by using three different graphemic patterns in English, do the following: Ask students one at a time to come to the board and write on it two or more one-syllable words apiece.

The following words might be written by them on the board:

the	meat	mouse	pot	feet	tan
home	book	five	poke	my	sleep
owl	cat	dig	ate	kill	pain
so	not	cute	wood	pun	oak
zoom	grape	pearl	eat	day	pig
pet	sat	moon	fat	owl	hit
big	tot	paw	boy	strip	cub
oink	cake	sly	me	one	fry
pick	thank	no	part	in	ball

Next, classify the words according to their vowel graphemic patterns. (Note that in a one-syllable word, there is one and only one vowel phoneme; therefore, there is one and only one vowel grapheme.)

Vowels—
Definitions

Single vowels		-vce	Vowel pairs	
Open syllable	Closed syllable			
the	pet part	home	owl	boy
so	big kill	grape	zoom	feet
sly	pick pun	cake	oink	day
no	cat strip	five	meat	owl
me	not in	cute	book	sleep
my	sat tan	poke	mouse	oak
fry	tot pig	ate	pearl	
	thank hit	one	moon	
	dig cub		paw	
	pot ball		wood	
	fat		eat	

Note: In *one* syllable words,

1. a single vowel in an open syllable often represents its own long sound ($y = /\bar{\imath}/$).

2. a single vowel in a closed syllable usually represents its own short sound.

3. if a word ends in a single-vowel-consonant-*e*, the *e* is silent, and often the vowel represents its own long sound.

4. the sounds that vowel pairs represent vary according to the precise vowel pair.

Vowels—
Definitions

SINGLE VOWEL GRAPHEMES[8]

Single vowels appear in closed and open syllables. The most common sounds they represent are given below.

1. *Closed Syllable* (a syllable that contains a single vowel and ends with a consonant): A single vowel in a closed syllable represents its own short sound, its *r* controlled sound when it is followed by an r, or a schwa sound.

2. *Open Syllable* (a syllable that contains a single vowel in a final position): If the single vowel in an open syllable is an *e, o,* or *u,* it usually represents its own long sound; if the vowel is an *a,* it may represent a schwa—53%, a *long a* sound—32%, or a *short a* sound—12%; if the vowel is *i,* it may represent a *schwa*—49%, a *short i* sound—37%, a *long i* sound—14% of the time.

3. *Single vowel generalization.* It may be simplest and wisest to teach: A single vowel may represent its own short sound, long sound, *r* controlled sound, or schwa. Teach students to try one sound, then another, until oral recognition is achieved. (For phonics to be useful—a triple associate skill—it is assumed that the student knows the word orally.)

Single Vowels

Examples

a) Short sounds

cap	bed	h*i*t	pot	mug
back	blest	p*i*ck	snob	trump
avid	asset	*i*nch	odd	utter
act	etch	*i*nk	optic	uncle

b) Long sounds

angel	senior	w*i*ld	scold	puny
cable	ego	b*i*nd	cozy	unite
basin	me	p*i*nt	coma	humid
saving	legal	v*i*sor	t oll	impugn

---

[8] See Appendix B.

c) *r* modified sounds

car	era	fire	sworn	lurid
stare	hero	fir	for	purity
lariat	her	irrigate	port	fury
arrogant	period	direct	floral	further

d) Schwa

aglow	dowel	peril	abbot	status
abyss	ripen	charity	atom	exodus
era	camel	janitor	bacon	circus
extra	comedy	vanity	pilot	upon

4. *Final y.* If a word ends with a *consonant* + *y*, the *y* will represent a *long i* sound if the word is monosyllabic; but the *y* will represent a *short i* (*long e*) sound if the word is polysyllabic. Examples are:

a) Monosyllabic words (*long i*)

my	thy	fry	shy	spry
by	dry	ply	sky	thy
cry	fly	pry	sly	try
why	wry			

b) Polysyllabic words (*short i*, or *long e*)

ably	candy	dingy	enemy	melody
academy	carry	ditty	fifty	mercy
acuity	crusty	elegy	hazy	rocky
agony	curly	empty	heavy	shady

Single
Vowels

FINAL VOWEL - CONSONANT - E[9]

When a word ends with a single vowel, single consonant, and an *e*, the *e* is silent, and the vowel usually represents its own long sound. Examples are:

1. Grapheme - phoneme relations for final vowel - consonant - *e:*

   a) Contrast word without *e* with word with *e*:

hat	hate	pet	Pete	bit	bite
mat	mate	let	complete	fir	fire
man	mane	met	mete	dim	dime
can	cane	them	theme	bid	bide
pan	pane	pet	compete	fin	fine

hop	hope	cut	cute
cop	cope	us	use
cod	code	cub	cube
mod	mode	purr	pure
nod	node	hug	huge

   b) Longer words:

lemonade	extreme	supine	compose	perfume
cavalcade	concede	imbibe	parole	misuse
awake	obsolete	combine	trombone	commute
detonate	velocipede	vaporize	zygote	tribune

Final v-c-*e*

2. Exceptions

   a) There are 68 primary-level words which are exceptions to this generalization. They are:

   a-e: have; are; purchase; aver*age*, cour*age*, man*age*, mess*age*, pass*age*, vill*age*, advant*age*; surface, palace; senate, separate

   e-e: there, where; were; college

---

[9] Lou E. Burmeister, "Final Vowel-Consonant-E," *The Reading Teacher* 24 (February 1971): 439-442.

i-e: live, give, office, active, notice, native, justice, practice, service, promise, examine, favorite, determine, opposite, representative; machine, magazine, police, automobile; engine

o-e: purpose, welcome; lose, improve, move, movement; remove, whose; gone; above, come, become, done, love, lovely, none, some, something, sometimes, somewhat, somewhere; one

u-e: rule, conclude, include; measure, pleasure, treasure; sure, assure

(Within these, there may be some dialectial variations, especially with the *u-e* words.)

b)   Groups of exceptions in more difficult words are (1) *i-e* words in which the *i* represents a *short i* sound: l*i*ve, g*i*ve, off*i*ce, prom*i*se; (2) *i-e* words in which the *i* represents a *long e* sound: mar*i*ne, magaz*i*ne; (3) *a-e* words in which the *a* represents a *short i* sound, especially -*ace*, -*age*, -*ate* words: surf*a*ce, pal*a*ce; aver*a*ge, cour*a*ge; sen*a*te, delic*a*te. Examples:

1)   Final *i-e* words, in which *i* represents a *short i* sound:

l*i*ve	impass*i*ve	decis*i*ve	off*i*ce
g*i*ve	impress*i*ve	evas*i*ve	prom*i*se
aggress*i*ve	mass*i*ve	respons*i*ve	bod*i*ce
express*i*ve	miss*i*ve	reflex*i*ve	avar*i*ce

2)   Final *i-e* words, in which *i* represents a *long e* sound:

el*i*te	mach*i*ne	pet*i*te	reg*i*me
figur*i*ne	magaz*i*ne	pol*i*ce	rout*i*ne
gabard*i*ne	mar*i*ne	rav*i*ne	val*i*se

3)   Final *a-e* words, in which *a* represents a *short i* sound:

surf*a*ce	aver*a*ge	sen*a*te
pal*a*ce	cour*a*ge	delic*a*te
popul*a*ce	ad*a*ge	ag*a*te
furn*a*ce	break*a*ge	priv*a*te
pref*a*ce	cabb*a*ge	clim*a*te

Final
v-c-*e*

★ VOWEL PAIRS[10]

There is no generalization that can be taught to cover a majority of instances of vowel pair grapheme to phoneme relationships. A particular generalization, however, may be taught to cover specific vowel pairs. The vowel pairs listed below need description in a phonics program.

grapheme-phoneme relations for vowel pairs

1. *First Vowel Long, Second Vowel Silent*
   a) If the vowel pair is *ai*, *ay*, *ee*, *ey*, or *oa*, usually the first vowel represents its own long sound, and the second vowel is silent.

$ai = /\bar{a}/$		$ay = /\bar{a}/$	
main	brain	pay	may
abstain	fail	hay	pray
gain	train	midway	stray
remain	sail	tray	play
waif	paint	fray	crayon
bail	mail	decay	essay

$ee = /\bar{e}/$		$ey = /\bar{e}/$ (or $/\breve{\imath}/$)	
meet	green	alley	money
beef	jeep	chimney	trolley
sleep	teeth	donkey	jockey
wheel	speech	monkey	jersey
newsreel	sheep	hockey	honey
cheek	weed	valley	kidney

$oa = /\bar{o}/$			
oak	coach	goat	foam
oar	boat	foal	boast
afloat	roast	soap	toad

Vowel Pairs

---

[10] See Appendix C. If a vowel pair grapheme occurred at least fifty times in the 17,310 most common English words, its most common sound, or sounds, are given in this section. This excludes *ew*, whose sounds vary greatly from dialect to dialect within the United States.

b) The most common sound the vowel pairs *ea* and *ow* represent is first vowel long, second vowel silent. But both pairs also have another common sound:

ea = /ē/		*ea* = /ĕ/	
meat	beach	bread	heavy
eaves	cheap	ahead	weather
steam	gleam	dead	leather
steal	beast	weapon	dread
weaver	yeast	wealth	sweater
least	squeal	dread	thread

ow = /ō/		*ow* = /ou/	
snow	flow	cow	flower
own	grow	town	vowel
rowboat	crow	powder	gown
gallows	hollow	owl	tower
mow	borrow	brown	eyebrow
slow	arrow	chow	plow

2. *Diphthongs*

a) The vowel pairs *oi* and *oy* represent the diphthong /oi/:

oi = /oi/	*oy* = /oi/
coin	toy
poison	oyster
boil	joy
moist	boy

Vowel
Pairs

b) The vowel pairs *ou* and *ow* represent the diphthong /ou/, but they also represent other sounds:

ou = /ou/	*ou* = /ə/	*ow* = /ou/	*ow* = /ō/
mouse	dangerous	cow	snow
south	leprous	town	own
proud	various	powder	rowboat
loud	joyous	owl	escrow
ground	envious	brown	stow

3. *Broad a* (circumflex *o*)[11] The vowel pairs *au* and *aw* represent the *broad a* sound, just as does *a* when followed by *ll* :

au = /ô/	aw = /ô/	a = /ô/
auto	awful ·	ball
fault	lawn	call
pauper	claw	fall
maul	straw	small

4. *Long and Short oo.* The vowel pair *oo* represents two sounds:

oo = /o͞o/		oo = /o͝o/	
rooster	lagoon	book	hooky
maroon	coon	shook	fishhook
pantaloon	toadstool	wool	wormwood
baboon	balloon	brook	woodchuck
cocoon	loon	football	cooky
spoon	groom	woolen	hood

5. *Ei and Ie.* The most common sound *ei* represents is *long a*. Otherwise *ei* and *ie* frequently represent the *long e* sound.

ei = /ā/	ei = /ē/	ie = /ē/
neighbor	ceiling	brief
sleigh	conceit	chief
reindeer	deceit	field
beige	receipt	fiend
weigh	seize	grief
eight	perceive	priest
seine	leisure	shield
veil	receive	thief

Vowel Pairs

---

[11] The symbol ô, called *circumflex o*, is the symbol used by most dictionaries to describe the most common sound of a *long o before an r*, e.g., fore (fôr), form (fôrm), fork (fôrk). It is also the symbol used to describe the most common sound *au* and *aw* represent, obviously in some American dialects the same sound as in fore, form, and fork, etc. Note these markings from a popular and reputable dictionary: auto (ô′to), fault (fôlt), awful (ô′ fəl), lawn (lôn), as well as ball (bôl), call (kôl). In the General American dialect, *broad a* seems to be a more appropriate term to use for the most common phoneme for the graphemes *au* and *aw* and *a* when followed by *ll*.

★ CONSONANTIZING OF *i*

When *io* or *ia* follows *c*, *t*, or *s*, the consonant plus the *i* combine to represent an /sh/ or /zh/ sound: racial, social, mention, caution; pension, mansion; vision, fusion.

ci = /sh/

crucial	social
facial	spacious
glacial	racial
special	musician
official	vicious

ti = /sh/

action	partial
adoption	initial
caution	mention
dictionary	convention
aviation	vacation

si = /sh/

mansion	conversion
pension	ascension
extension	intension
tension	dimension
expansion	

si = /zh/

erosion
fusion
television
decision
illusion

PART III

Particularly Useful Grapheme to Phoneme Relationships

Phonic Syllabication[12]

A. Determination of a syllable

B. Syllabication generalizations

---

[12] Phonic syllabication generalizations are used only when morphological syllabication generalizations do not apply (prefix/root or root/root or root/suffix).

★ DETERMINATION OF A SYLLABLE

There is one, and only one, vowel phoneme (sound) in a syllable, and there is one, and only one, vowel grapheme (symbol) in a syllable. Vowel graphemes are (a) single vowels—c*a*p, m*e*, b*a*by; (b) vowel pairs, or clusters—m*ai*n, r*ou*nd, b*eau*tiful; or (c) a final vowel-(consonant)-e—c*a*k*e*, P*e*t*e*, h*o*m*e*.

Methodology for teaching students in the middle grades and above follows.

☐ **Auditory Discrimination.** Ask students, one at a time, to give you some one-syllable words. Ask them how many vowel sounds are in each word. Next ask for two-syllable words and the number of vowel sounds in each. Then ask for three-syllable words and the number of vowel sounds in each.

☐ **Auditory Discrimination Exercise.** Ask students to number from 1 to 25 on a piece of paper. Using the list of words below, the teacher first reads the number, followed by the word. The teacher hesitates long enough to allow the students to record the number of syllables in the word. Then the teacher goes on to the next word, etc. Students *do not* see these words in print.

1. November	10. thousand	19. Mississippi
2. elephant	11. compete	20. moon
3. automobile	12. campus	21. astronaut
4. Spain	13. reading	22. poodle
5. red	14. pie	23. mountain
6. octopus	15. Pacific	24. cake
7. football	16. twenty	25. lemon
8. basketball	17. Germany	
9. Chicago	18. spider	

The teacher checks each paper and notes which students have made errors. Any student making more than three errors needs special help.

Determination of Syllables

☐ **Visual Discrimination Exercise.** Next, the teacher writes the same 25 words on the board—or distributes a copy of them—and explains that each time there is a *single vowel*, a *vowel pair or cluster*, or a final *vowel-consonant-e*, there is a syllable.

Students are asked to circle each vowel grapheme. (A vowel grapheme is composed of the number of vowels it takes to spell an unbroken vowel sound. Usually, English vowel graphemes are spelled with *one vowel*, as in dog, hi, and champ, or with *vowel pairs*, as in see, toast, pay, and each, or with a vowel and a final *e*, separated by a consonant, as in bake, hope, tide, and use.)

Answers

1. N(o)v(e)m b(e)r
2. (e)l(e)p h(a)n t
3. (a u) t(o)m(o)b(i)l(e)
4. S p(a i)n
5. r(e)d
6. (o)c t(o)p(u)s
7. f(o o)t b(a)l l
8. b(a)s k(e)t b(a)l l
9. C h(i)c(a)g(o)
10. t h(o u)s(a)n d
11. c(o)m p(e)t(e)
12. c(a)m p(u)s
13. r(e a)d(i)n g

14. p(i e)
15. P(a)c(i)f(i)c
16. t w(e)n t(y)
17. G(e)r m(a)n(y)
18. s p(i)d(e)r
19. M(i)s s(i)s s(i)p p(i)
20. m(o o)n
21. (a)s t r(o)n(a u)t
22. p(o o)d l(e)
23. m(o u)n t(a i)n
24. c(a)k(e)
25. l(e)m(o)n

☐ **Hypothetical Words Exercise.** Next, students are given "hypothetical words" and are asked to circle each vowel grapheme and write the number of syllables the word contains (visual discrimination).

Determination of Syllables

v = vowel   c = consonant   l = l   e = e

1. c v c v v c _____
2. v v c v c v v _____
3. c c v c v c e _____
4. v c v c l e _____

5. c v c c v v c e _____   16. c v c l e   _____
6. v c v c c l e _____   17. v v c v c   _____
7. c v c v c c   _____   18. c c v   _____
8. v c e   _____   19. v c c   _____
9. c c v c c   _____   20. c v c e   _____
10. c v v c c v   _____   21. v v c v v c c v c e _____
11. c c c c v   _____   22. c v c c v v c c c   _____
12. v c   _____   23. v c l e   _____
13. v c c v c c   _____   24. c v c v c v c   _____
14. c v v c v c l e _____   25. c v c c v c c v c c _____
15. v c v v c c c _____

Answers

v = vowel   c = consonant   1 = 1   e = e

1. c(v)c(v v)c   2   14. c(v v)c(v)c'l(e)   3
2. (v v)c(v)c(v v)   3   15. (v)c(v v)c c c   2
3. c c(v)c(v)c(e)   2   16. c(v)c'l(e)   2
4. (v)c(v)c'l(e)   3   17. (v v)c(v)c   2
5. c(v)c c(v v)c(e)   2   18. c c(v)   1
6. (v)c(v)c c'l(e)   3   19. (v)c c   1
7. c(v)c(v)c c   2   20. c(v)c(e)   1
8. (v)c(e)   1   21. (v v)c(v v)c c(v)c(e)   3
9. c c(v)c c   1   22. c(v)c c(v v)c c c   2
10. c(v v)c c(v)   2   23. (v)c'l(e)   2
11. c c c c(v)   1   24. c(v)c(v)c(v)c   3
12. (v)c   1   25. c(v)c c(v)c c(v)c c   3
13. (v)c c(v)c c   2

Determination of Syllables

☐ **Nonsense Words Exercise.** Students are supplied with "nonsense words" and asked to circle each vowel grapheme, then write the number of syllables the word contains (visual discrimination).

1. a i m s e l _____
2. g o a p t u n _____
3. r i f d o l _____
4. y e a k b a x _____
5. o u c c y _____
6. m o i h o w _____
7. j e n t y _____
8. r e e v a n o _____
9. z o o g a w _____
10. a u m u f e _____
11. d i s t l e _____
12. y o i p o h e _____
13. v a b d o y _____
14. s o t h s i m e _____
15. a u k w i p _____
16. l o a s h o o _____
17. j e a p h c h e t _____
18. n a g e _____
19. n a i g e _____
20. w a n k l e _____
21. w a k l e _____
22. n e n a y _____
23. s p l o n k _____
24. s p l o n e _____
25. s c h w y _____

Answers

1. a i m s e l — 2
2. g o a p t u n — 2
3. r i f d o l — 2
4. y e a k b a x — 2
5. o u c c y — 2
6. m o i h o w — 2
7. j e n t y — 2
8. r e e v a n o — 3
9. z o o g a w — 2
10. a u m u f e — 2
11. d i s t l e — 2
12. y o i p o h e — 2
13. v a b d o y — 2
14. s o t h s i m e — 2
15. a u k w i p — 2
16. l o a s h o o — 2
17. j e a p h c h e t — 2
18. n a g e — 1
19. n a i g e — 1
20. w a n k l e — 2
21. w a k l e — 2
22. n e n a y — 2
23. s p l o n k — 1
24. s p l o n e — 1
25. s c h w y — 1

★ SYLLABICATION GENERALIZATIONS

There are three generalizations that explain where words are syllabicated in English. They are:

1. *Situation:* two vowel graphemes separated by two consonants (v c c v).

   When two vowel graphemes are separated by two consonants, we divide between the consonants: as-ter, sil-ver, tar-get but-ler.

   [It is suggested that words containing two like consonants between two vowel graphemes not be included in this generalization (except *cc* and *gg* when followed by *e*, *i*, or *y*) because only one sound is represented by these two consonants. Instead, words containing two like consonants might be included in the v c v generalization: rab(b)-it, car(r)-ot, ba-(l)loon, e-(s)say. However, published phonics programs are not yet this innovative.]

2. *Situation*: two vowel graphemes separated by a single consonant (v c v).

   When two vowel graphemes are separated by a single consonant, the consonant may go with the first or the second vowel. In primary level words, it is more likely to go with the first vowel; in more difficult words, it tends to go with the second vowel. At all levels, there is about a 45-55 split (liz-ard, lem-on, wag-on; ra-zor, spi-der, ti-ger).

3. *Situation*: word ending in a consonant-*l-e*

   When a word ends in a consonant-*l-e*, these three letters usually compose the final syllable (bi-ble, ea-gle, bun-dle, tur-tle, noo-dle).

Methodology for teaching students in the middle grades and above follows.

**Syllabication
Generalizations**

☐ **Syllabicating Hypothetical Words.** Ask students to divide the "hypothetical words" on pages 83-84 into syllables.

Answers

1. c(v)c, (v v)c [13] _____2_____
2. (v v)c, (v)c, (v v) _____3_____
3. c c(v)c, (v)c (e) _____2_____
4. (v)c, (v)/ c/l (e) _____3_____
5. c(v)c / c(v v)c (e) _____2_____
6. c(v)c, (v)c / c/l (e) _____3_____
7. c(v)c, (v)c c _____2_____
8. (v)c (e) _____1_____
9. c c(v)c c _____1_____
10. c(v v)c / c(v) _____2_____
11. c c c c(v) _____1_____
12. (v)c _____1_____
13. (v)c / c(v)c c _____2_____

14. c (v v)c, (v)/ c/l (e) _____3_____
15. (v)c, (v v)c c c _____2_____
16. c(v)/ c/l (e) _____2_____
17. (v v)c, (v)c _____2_____
18. c c(v) _____1_____
19. (v)c c _____1_____
20. c(v)c (e) _____1_____
21. (v v)c, (v v)c / c(v)c (e) _____3_____
22. c(v)c / c(v v)c c c _____2_____
23. (v)/ c/l (e) _____2_____
24. c(v)c, (v)c, (v)c _____3_____
25. c(v)c / c(v)c / c(v)c c _____3_____

---

[13] Use c, to indicate that the division may come before, or after, the single consonant (generalization 2, above).

☐ **Syllabicating Nonsense Words.** Ask the students to divide the nonsense words on page page 85 into syllables.

Answers

1. a i m/s e l	2	14. s o t h/s i m e [14]	2
2. g o a p/t u n	2	15. a u k/w i p	2
3. r i f/d o l	2	16. l o a s h, o o	2
4. y e a k/b a x	2	17. j e a p h/c h e t	2
5. o u c/c y	2	18. n a g e	1
6. m o i' h, o w	2	19. n a i g e	1
7. j e n/t y	2	20. w a n/k l e	2
8. r e e' v, a n, o	3	21. w a k' l e	2
9. z o o' g, a w	2	22. n e n, a y	2
10. a u' m, u f e	2	23. s p l o n k	1
11. d i s/t' l e	2	24. s p l o n e	1
12. y o i p, o h e	2	25. s c h w y	1
13. v a b/d o y	2		

☐ **Syllabicating Real Words.** Now we are ready for real words. To review the generalizations, write the following on the board:

Clue 1: vc-cv

tar-get	win-dow	for-got
vc-cv	vc-cv	vc-cv
per-fume	mem-ber	pub-lic
vc-cv	vc-cv	vc-cv

**Syllabication
Generalizations**

_____

[14] The following are digraphs (one sound spelled with two letters) and are never divided between: *ch, sh, th, ph.*

When two vowel sounds are separated by two consonants, divide between the consonants.

Clue 2: v-cv or vc-v

na-tion	sha-dow	ne-ver
v-cv	v-cv	v-cv
eth-ics	mag-ic	feath-er
vc-v	vc-v	vc-v

When two vowel sounds are separated by one consonant, divide either before or after the consonant. Try before the consonant first, and if you don't recognize the word, try dividing after the consonant.

Clue 3: -cle

ti-tle	bi-ble	bun-dle
-cle	-cle	-cle
ea-gle	can-dle	fa-ble
-cle	-cle	-cle

When a word ends in -cle, divide before the consonant.

Next, students are given real words. Ask them to divide these into syllables.

1. November
2. elephant
3. automobile
4. Spain
5. red
6. octopus
7. football
8. basketball
9. Chicago
10. thousand
11. compete
12. campus
13. reading
14. pie
15. Pacific
16. twenty
17. Germany
18. spider
19. Mississippi
20. moon
21. astronaut
22. poodle
23. mountain
24. cake
25. lemon

□ **Summary.** Ask students one at a time to come to the board and write several two-syllable words on the board. The following words might be written by them:

bookend	sugar	grapefruit	foreign
table	serpent	promptly	oatmeal
seven	either	button	zombie

Syllabication Generalizations

after	unkind	uncle	problem
monkey	about	hornet	going
airport	able	pumpkin	resort
yellow	gospel	appeal	perfect
nightly	viewpoint	success	Arab
silent	nature	parking	barley
mascot	council	human	simple

Next, ask students to classify these words according to the syllabication generalization they theoretically should follow, according to (a) morphology or (b) spelling pattern, i.e., phonics.

The words should be classified thus:

1. *morphological syllabication*

prefix/root	*root/root*	*root/suffix*
un/kind	book/end	night/ly
	air/port	prompt/ly
	view/point	park/ing
	grape/fruit	go/ing
	oat/meal	

2. *Phonic syllabication*

vc/cv		*v/cv* or *vc/v*[15]		*-cle*
af/ter	(*like cons.*)	si/lent	for/eign	ta/ble
mon/key	but/ton	ei/ther	ar/ab	un/cle
mas/cot	ap/peal	a/bout	sev/en	sim/ple
ser/pent	suc/cess	a/ble	sug/ar	
gos/pel	yel/low	na/ture		
coun/cil	or	hu/man		
hor/net	butt/on	re/sort		
pump/kin	a/ppeal			
zom/bie	yell/ow			
prob/lem				
per/fect				
bar/ley				

---

[15] It appears, to this writer at least, that there is no point in a reading program of splitting hairs over the exact point of syllabication, e.g., whether a word is syllabicated before or after the consonant. The important consideration is whether or not the reader *recognizes* the written word—not where it is syllabicated. Syllabication generalizations are taught to help readers associate the written word with its oral counterpart.

☐ **Follow Through.** When a real word is to be taught and it is phonetic:

1. Write it on the board, preferably in a sentence.
2. Ask the students to try to pronounce it.
3. If they cannot pronounce it, ask how many syllables it has and where the syllabic divisions are. Mark them on the board. Then ask students to pronounce it. If they cannot, do the following:
4. Reinforce appropriate vowel generalizations and/or consonant generalizations by listing several easy words that have the troublesome vowel or consonant grapheme.
5. Ask them to pronounce the word, or pronounce it for them, if necessary. Have them repeat it orally.
6. Define it, and/or use it in a sentence. Use an illustration if possible.

☐ **Syllabication—Words That May Give Students Some Trouble.** One of the more interesting aspects of diachronic linguistics relates to sound changes in our language. You may wish to refer to Chapter 2, p. 49, in which the consonant shift is described.

Today American English is undergoing an extremely important sound shift, though those of us who speak American English may not be aware of it, since most of us are participating in it. It's like not noticing how much a child is growing when we see him every day.

The present-day sound shift is this: Many words, particularly those that were formerly three-syllable words, are dropping an internal vowel phoneme and, thus, are dropping a syllable. Though the letter remains in the spelling, it now represents *no* phoneme.

For example, examine the following words:

om*e*let	fam*i*ly	av*e*rage	gen*e*ral
cath*o*lic	cam*e*ra	cab*i*net	lib*e*ral

Do *you* pronounce the italicized letters? Perhaps . . . perhaps not. Many Americans do not.

If we agree that phonic generalizations *describe*, rather than *prescribe*, what language is like (not what it ought to be like), teachers may have some problems here. Students will identify vowel graphemes (?) that have no phoneme counterparts.

Syllabication
Generalizations

There aren't just a few such words. There are *hundreds* of them! Here are some more:

interest	javelin	covenant
sovereign	bachelor	delivery
separate	cannery	diamond[16]
limerick	admiral	diary[16]
ivory	company	similar
caramel	cardinal	chicory
chocolate	insulin	sentinal
ovary	surgery	margarine
maverick	memory	mineral
misery	natural	monopoly
opera	easily	factory
gallery	history	insolent

Syllabication Generalizations

---

[16] *ia* is the only vowel pair in English that commonly describes two vowel sounds, rather than one: piano, giant, etc.

Teaching Phonics

The teaching of a phonic principle requires four steps:

1. auditory discrimination
2. visual discrimination
3. blending—analytic (grapheme substitution), or synthetic
4. contextual application

Explanation of Steps

In *auditory discrimination* a check is made to determine whether the learner can orally identify the sound represented by the grapheme being taught. Often the children are asked to clap whenever the sound is spoken in a word, and perhaps in a certain position in the word, and to raise their hands if the sound does not occur in the spoken word. Children who respond incorrectly are easily identified and are then given extra help.

For example, the teacher may ask the children to show the green side of a card when a *short a sound* occurs in a list of words such as the following, which she reads, and to show the red side when it does not occur: cat, fat, head, ban, tad, put. The child who shows the green side when *head* or *put* is said, and the child who shows the red side when *cat* or *fat* or *ban* or *tad* is said probably needs extra help in auditory discrimination of the *short a* sound.

Visual discrimination often accompanies—or directly precedes or follows—auditory discrimination. The child being taught

93

about the sound which *d* represents in an initial position may work along with the teacher in composing a chart such as this:

d	*D*
*d*og	*D*ick
*d*ig	*D*ad
*d*ock	*D*olly
*d*irty	*D*orothy
*d*raw	*D*onald
*d*rill	*D*aisy

When we work with whole words (as above)—or with even larger units, such as phrases and sentences—the approach is termed *analytical*.

When working on *blending* using an analytic (word) approach, the teacher commonly uses a type of CLOZE technique, in which one grapheme in a word is deleted and others are substituted. For example:

bat → _at → *h*at or *c*at or *f*at

or

bat → ba_ → ba*d* or ba*g* or ba*n*

or

bat → b_t → b*e*t or b*i*t or b*u*t or b*oa*t or b*ee*t or b*ea*t

Another analytic "blending" approach utilizes sentences. The following is a morphological, not phonic, approach:

The boy is   jumping
The boy is   _____ing.
              *sing*ing.
               *go*ing.
               *act*ing.

Other approaches are synthetic in nature:

$/k/ + /\breve{a}/ + /t/$ = cat; $/r/ + /\breve{a}/ + /t/$ = rat (phonic)
C + A + T = cat; R + A + T = rat (alphabetic)

Contextual application is necessary to assure that meaning is attached to the spoken or written word. Once a word is recognized through the use of phonics, the teacher assures herself that meaning is related to it by asking the child to use it in a meaning-ful sentence or by using it thus herself. Pictures, real objects, or experiences may also be used to clarify meaning.

On the other hand, perhaps the word was phonically analyzed because it appeared in context. Demonstrating that the triple-associate relationship exists completes the teaching-learning circle.

On the pages that follow, classwide, group, and individual activities are explained to give the teacher some ideas of how phonics might be taught. These activities are meant to introduce and/or supplement the teaching of phonics in a carefully sequenced program. Also, these activities would be useful for a corrective or remedial program. In such a case, the teacher should know exactly what weaknesses a child has. She should then teach the child in these specific areas of weakness.

Each activity suggested in this chapter is designed to teach at least one of the above components of a phonics lesson, while many activities include all four.

This chapter presents activities for teaching phonics in the following order:

I.   Consonants

    A.   Single consonants

        1.   Initial position

        2.   Final position

        3.   The consonants *c* and *g*

    B.   Double consonants (or consonant clusters)

        1.   Consonant blends and digraphs

        2.   Silent consonants

II. Vowels

    A.   Single vowels

    B.   Final vowel-consonant-*e*

    C.   Vowel pairs

III. Syllabication

SINGLE CONSONANTS — INITIAL POSITION

☐ **Names Game.** The teacher refers to her class list. On separate slips of paper for each appropriate single consonant, she records the first or last name of each student whose first or last name begins with that consonant. Some slips may look like these:

B		D		M	
Betty	Bailey	Dorothy	Dover	Mary	Mason
Barbara	Brown	Daniel	Durango		
		David			

She puts the slips in a hat for the following activity:

1. The teacher draws out a slip and reads the letter.
2. Children whose first name begins with that letter stand up.
3. Children whose last name begins with that letter clap their hands.
4. By referring to the names on the paper, the teacher can check to see if the appropriate children are responding. (Some may *both* stand up and clap their hands, if both names begin with the same consonant.)

Another activity:

1. The teacher draws out a slip and says, I'm thinking of a name that begins like Bob (a name not on the slip).
2. Children raise their hands if they can name a child in the class whose name begins with a *B*.
3. The teacher calls on a child to give the name, or names.
4. The teacher observes which children find this difficult and gives them special help.

☐ **Five Teams.** The teacher counts children off thus: 1, 2, 3, 4, 5—1, 2, 3, 4, 5—1, 2, 3, 4, 5—1, 2, 3, 4, 5,—etc., until each child has a number. Children with the same number form a team. The activity proceeds thus:

1. The child who was the first one to be given the number by the teacher is the team leader.

2. The chalkboard is divided into five areas, one area given to each team. The leader is asked to write the first consonant in his or her name at the top of his team's area. Thus Peter would write "*p*" and Alice would write "*l*." The leader is asked to write a word on the board that begins with that letter.

3. Each child opens a book he or she is reading to a page designated by the teacher. He finds words on that page, or pages following, that begin with his team's letter and writes them on the board.

4. The team with the largest number of words on the board wins.

5. Children then pronounce at least some of the words and learn to use them in sentences.

□   **Discriminate and Eliminate.** The teacher writes a list of words on the board, for example:

house	mouse	ham	paper	foot
hello	hollow	baby	goat	holiday
queen	begin	help	pumpkin	habit

1. The teacher says, "Who can erase one word that doesn't begin like *honey*?" (For another list a word beginning with a different consonant would be used.)

2. The game is over when all words that don't begin with "*h*" are erased.

□   **Make a Wordo Card.** The teacher gives each child an 8 1/2 × 11" sheet of paper.

1. The child is asked to fold it lengthwise in half and then in half again. He has a long strip then, and folds that in half and then in half again. When he opens the paper, he has sixteen rectangles.

2. Using 16 of the following 17 letters—b, d, f, h, j, k, l, m, n, p, r, s, t, v, w, y, z—in random order, the teacher says words which begin with each letter.

3. When the teacher says a word, each child writes the letter which represents the initial sound in one of the rectangles. When finished, every rectangle should have a different letter in it.

Single Consonants— Consistent

☐   **Play Wordo.** The teacher has 16 words in a hat, each word beginning with one of the consonant letters used for making the Wordo cards.

1. The teacher takes a word out of the hat, says it, and the children cover the letter on their card which represents the initial sound in the word.
2. The teacher and children continue thus until someone calls out "Wordo." To call out Wordo, the child must have covered four letters, either diagonally, vertically, or horizontally.
3. The child who has correctly called out "Wordo" most often wins for the day.

☐   **I Spy.** The teacher says, "I see something that begins with the same sound as *pink*." The child who responds first by giving the name of an object in the room—like *pillow* or *pumpkin*—says, "I see something that begins with the same sound as _____." The child who first responds correctly continues, etc.

☐   **Jingles.** The teacher has some two-line jingles such as the following:

We have a big cat—
It would like to eat a big __at.   (to teach *r*)

We have a big cat—
Our cat is __at.   (to teach *f*)

We have a big cat—
It sleeps on a __at.   (to teach *m*)

We have a big cat—
For Christmas it wears a red __at.   (to teach *h*)

Procedure

1. The teacher reads one jingle at a time, except for the last word.
2. The children supply the last word.
3. The teacher writes *cat* on the board. Under it, she writes the word given by the children, e.g., *rat*.
4. She draws a chart on the board, such as the following.

r	R
rat	

5. She asks children for other words that begin like rat and fills them in on the chart, for example:

r	R
rat	Robert
ran	Raymond
rain	
rabbit	
round	

6. The children compose a short story using these words, and the teacher writes it on the board, as in the Language Experience approach. For example:

> Robert and Raymond ran in the rain
> to catch a round rabbit and a fat rat.

☐ **Picture Sorting.** From magazines, cut out a set of pictures, the names of some of which begin with the consonant being taught. Have the children (or one child) sort the pictures into two piles, one with pictures that begin with that consonant, and the other pile that does not.

If the teacher has enough pictures, this activity can be engaged in many ways. For example:

1. The children sort the pictures into three piles: (1) pictures that begin with, for example, *m*; (2) pictures that begin with *n*; (3) other pictures.

2. Or, *b, p, t,* others. Etc., etc.

☐ **Pocket Chart.** The teacher slips magazine pictures in a large pocket chart and gives a child multiple copies of one, two, or possibly more consonant letters plus blank cards. The child slips in the appropriate consonant letter for the initial sound of each picture and slips in a blank card for pictures which do not begin with sounds represented by the letters he has been given.

SINGLE CONSONANTS — FINAL POSITION

Single
Consonants—
Consistent

☐   **Baseball.** The teacher marks homeplate and the three bases for a diamond on the floor in the room. To do this, she might use bricks, mats, or even chairs. The class is divided into two teams.

1. The teacher serves as "pitcher." She says a word, such as *bean.*

2. The "batter" must give four words ending with *n* to make a homerun. If he gives one, he goes to first base, two to second, three to third. He is "out" if he can name none. There are no strikes.

3. The next "batter" is given another word. No bases can be stolen, but the "batter" can help his teammate take bases by responding correctly.

4. Three outs, and the other team gets its turn.

5. Nine innings?

☐   **Stand Up.** The teacher passes out word cards to the class. She asks children to stand up if the word on their card ends like a word she says. Variation: Each child has several cards. They hold up the card that ends like the word she says.

☐   **Change a Letter.** The teacher writes words on the board that with a final letter change could spell another word. If the teacher were teaching final *t*, the following words might be on the board:

    hum   pen   fan   cob

1. The teacher writes sentences, such as the following, on the board:
    a)   I wish I could live in a grass _____.
    b)   Juan had a dog for a _____.
    c)   In our tent we slept on a _____.

2. The teacher reads the words to the class. Then she reads sentence (a). She asks the class which word with the last letter (or sound) changed would fit in the blank.

3. The child who responds *hum* is correct. She asks him what the correct word is. He should say *hut.*

4. The teacher writes *hut* under *hum*, says the two words, then reads the sentence with the word *hut* in it.

5. She proceeds in a like manner with the other sentences.

6. Then she draws a chart on the board like the following:

-t
hut
pet
cot

7. She asks children to suggest words that end like *hut*, *pet*, and *cot*. She writes these on the chart, for example, cat, hat, wet, dot, fit, it, at, not, nut, etc.

8. She points out that these words end with the same letter and with the same sound.

☐ **Rummy.** Using 3 × 5" cards the teacher makes a deck of 32 cards. Four cards are made for each of eight books. Each book is composed of words whose initial and middle letters are the same but whose final letters vary. For example:

1. hat   ham   had   has
2. pen   pet   peg   pep
3. sit   sip   sin   six
4. top   tot   tom   ton
5. cub   cup   cut   cud
6. cap   can   cab   cat
7. bit   big   bid   bin
8. cob   cot   cod   cog

Directions

1. Play like rummy. Deal four cards to each child.[1] When it is his turn, the child draws a card from the pile or may take the "exposed" card pile if he has two cards of the book the top card is part of. When he has a book, he lays it down if he can use each word in a sentence. He discards a card face up.

2. The first child to be out of cards wins. Or make the rules as you wish.

---

[1] With a short deck it is best for only two or three children to play.

☐   **Variation of Rummy.** Use the same technique as above, but have two cards per book, with a total of 52 cards. Any number up to eight can play. To put a book down, the child must be able to pronounce the words and use them in a sentence. The following books might be used:

1.	pen	– pet	14.	not	– nod
2.	top	– tot	15.	rod	– rob
3.	cub	– cut	16.	sob	– sod
4.	hat	– ham	17.	tan	– tab
5.	cob	– cot	18.	web	– wed
6.	six	– sit	19.	vat	– van
7.	big	– bit	20.	kid	– kit
8.	pat	– pan	21.	jab	– jam
9.	dig	– dip	22.	hid	– him
10.	pot	– pop	23.	fin	– fig
11.	hop	– hot	24.	cat	– cab
12.	fan	– fat	25.	bat	– bag
13.	mob	– mop	26.	tap	– tab

SINGLE CONSONANTS — *c* AND *g*

□ **Spelldown.** On the board the teacher writes words which begin with a *c* or *g*, but with the *c* or *g* omitted, for example:

(*c*)ab	(*g*)olf	(*g*)lobe	(*g*)em
(*g*)as	(*c*)ake	(*c*)ent	(*c*)eiling
(*g*)lass	(*g*)iant	(*g*)leeful	(*g*)erm
(*c*)all	(*g*)um	(*c*)ap	(*c*)at
(*g*)low	(*c*)ell	(*g*)entle	(*c*)up
(*c*)olt	(*g*)un	(*g*)arbage	(*g*)enie
(*g*)asoline	(*g*)reen	(*c*)ity	(*c*)ircus
(*c*)ereal	(*c*)ow	(*c*)ar	(*g*)ypsy

c and g

1. The children form into two teams.

2. In a hat the teacher has the exact number of cards of the following types to complete the words on the board:

    c is soft – /s/
    c is hard – /k/
    g is soft – /j/
    g is hard – /g/

    She draws a card and reads it. For example, she reads "soft *c*" or "hard *c*," or she may read "*c* as in city" or "*c* as in cat."

3. Play like Spelldown, with the child going to the board and filling in the blank in order to score for his team. He must also say the word and use it in a sentence.

□ **Crossword Puzzle.** Compose crossword puzzles such as the following, using words that have *c*'s or *g*'s in them. Have soft *c* (or soft *g*) words run one way and hard *c* (or hard *g*) words run the other way. For the *c* puzzle, write in all the *c*'s and for the *g* puzzle, write in all the *g*'s. Clues to the words, besides the definitions, would be the possible range of letters that might follow the *c* or *g*. For example, if the *c* or *g* is soft, it would be followed by *e*, *i*, or *y*. If it's hard, it would not be followed by *e*, *i*, or *y*, but could be followed by almost any other letter, especially *a*, *o*, *u*, *c*, *k*, or *r* if it's a hard *c*—or *a*, *o*, *u*, *g*, *l*, *n*, or *r* if it's a hard *g*. Or the *c* or *g* would be in the final position in the word.

C Puzzle

c and g

Across: (all hard c's)
- 4. small vacation house
- 5. freight
- 6. large black bird
- 9. sharp and clear, brittle
- 12. shrub with purple flowers
- 13. region near North Pole
- 14. ice cream holder
- 15. a favorite candy
- 16. a crafty procedure
- 19. one goes to school to get it
- 22. concealed
- 23. sea creature with bony shell
- 26. a birthday treat
- 27. a sweet thing
- 28. a large fortified building

Down: (all soft c's)
- 1. a school subject
- 2. a cereal grass, favorite cereal
- 3. we speak with it
- 5. a grain used as food
- 7. unforeseen happening
- 8. a role of tobacco leaf
- 10. chief school official
- 11. a water fixture
- 17. calm, quiet state
- 18. small cube used in playing games
- 20. agreeable
- 21. move to music
- 22. area in which we exist
- 24. a hundredth part of a dollar
- 25. highest playing card

G Puzzle

c and g

Across (all hard g's)

2. heroic narrative
4. Indian hut
8. instrument used to measure earth vibration
10. a favorite string instrument
11. U.S. legislative body
12. ingredient used for sweetening
14. freight
16. clutch
20. transparent substance used in windows
21. amusement activity
22. to equip with sails
23. to hang loosely and swing
25. to move smoothly
27. a Spanish-American dance
28. Eskimo house
29. to refuse to take notice of

Down (all soft g's)

1. a favorite cake
3. How old are you? What's your_____?
5. a machine
6. an extremely large person
7. seasoned meat in a skin
9. porous masses
13. science concerned with preserving the environment
15. come into view
17. a spiritual being
18. stamps for mailing
19. a shortened version
23. exposure to injury
24. a nomad
26. a likeness of a person or thing

☐   **Seatword Activity.** For students at about the fourth-grade level and above, see exercises on pages [57–61] of this book.

☐   **Team Work.** Divide the class into five or six teams. Ask each child to select a book and take it with him to his team center. (This book should be at the third-grade level or above if it contains a controlled vocabulary.)

c and *g*

1. Have each team select one person to serve as a scribe. The scribe is given a sheet of paper with the following written on it:

c as in city	*c* as in cat
1.	1.
2.	2.
3.	3.
•	•
•	•
•	•
25.	25.

2. Each child pages through his book, looking for words that contain *c*'s (omit *ch*). When a child finds such a word, he spells it for the scribe and tells the scribe which column it is to be written in.

3. After a specified amount of time—about ten minutes—the teacher calls time. The team with the most words wins this part of the game.

4. Next the teacher asks the teams to list, after each word, the letter that follows the *c*.

5. Then the teacher asks the team members to formulate a generalization for the pronunciation of words that contain *c*'s. The first team that formulates the generalization wins this part of the game.

6. Next the teacher writes a word that contains a *c* on the board. She asks for volunteers to pronounce it. Next she asks that it be used in a sentence. She continues in this way with 12 – 20 words.

7. The same activity could be used with *g* words.

DOUBLE CONSONANTS — BLENDS AND DIGRAPHS

☐ **Pantomiming.** The teacher tells the children that she is going to ask someone to act out the meaning of a word that begins with *gl*. She whispers the word *glad* to a child. The others guess the word. Other words that might be used are: glide, glass, globe, gloom. Other blends could also be used, e.g., *gr*: grin, grow, green, greet; *fl*: fly, flag, flow; etc.

The same technique can be used with consonant digraphs, such as: thief, throw, there, photo, phone, chill, chicken, chief.

☐ **Add a Letter and Make a Blend.** The teacher writes words like the following on the board and makes sure the children can pronounce these words.

wing	low	peak	lad
law	rim	tare	lag

1. Then the teacher writes sentences such as the following on the board:

   a)   Mary played on the __ wing.

   b)   It is not polite to __ tare.

   c)   We pledge allegiance to our __ lag.

   d)   Harry was __ lad to go to the party.

   Etc.

2. The children are asked to add a letter so the sentence makes sense. The first child who can goes to the board and adds the consonant.

3. When all sentences are completed, the teacher writes each of the new words on the board. For example:

   *sw*ing   *st*are   *fl*ag   *gl*ad

4. She underlines the blend, and asks the children to suggest other words that begin with the same blends. She writes each under the corresponding word.

☐ **Add a Digraph.** The teacher writes words like the following on the board:

ant   is   ill   ink   row

1. The teacher writes sentences such as the following on the board:

   a)   The cold mouse developed a __ ill.

   b)   What do you __ink we should do?

   c)   Should we __row the mouse out?

   d)   __is is what Marie suggested.

   e)   Let's sing a __ant to him.

2. The children are asked to add a digraph (*sh*, *ph*, *ch*, or *th*) so the sentence makes sense. The first child who can goes to the board and writes in the digraph.

3. When all sentences are completed, the teacher writes each of the new words on the board. For example:

   chill   think   this
   chant   throw

4. She underlines the digraph, and asks the children to suggest other words that begin with the same digraph. She writes each under the corresponding word.

Double Consonants— Blends and Digraphs

DOUBLE CONSONANTS — SILENT CONSONANTS

☐ **Cross Out.** The teacher lists words on the board that have silent consonants in them, e.g.:

knee	cannon	design	wrong
raccoon	patch	balloon	lodge
psalm	pillow	comb	common

Children come to the board to cross out the silent letter.

☐ **Another Word.** In a hat the teacher puts slips of paper, each having on it a word with a silent letter. The class is divided into two teams for a spelldown. A child draws a slip, reads the word, and tells what letter is silent. For this he scores one point for his team. He scores another point if he can give another word with the same letter silent. The team with the highest score wins.

Silent
Consonants

SINGLE VOWELS

☐ **Short A Words.** Teach *short a* words using pictures. For example:

map	cat	hat
cap	fan	pan

Single Vowels

Next, cut the words off of the pictures. Insert the picture cards in a pocket chart, and deal the word cards to the children. Have each child in turn insert his word card in the chart along with the appropriate picture. This activity can be used for any short vowel.

☐ **Cloze.** To teach *short i* words, after having taught *short a* words, use sentences such as the following:

1. John wore a *hat*.
   He h__t the ball.   (hat→h__t→hit)
2. Mom had a *pan* on the stove.
   When Dad bowled, he hit only one p__n. (pan→p__n→pin)
3. Mary had a *fan* in her hand.
   She saw a fish with a f__n.   (fan→f__n→fin)

When children respond with the correct word, write the *i* in the word, using colored chalk. Other pairs of words that could be used are: bag-big, bat-bit, dad-did, has-his, mad-mid, pat-pit, crab-crib, draft-drift, lamp-limp, lamb-limb.

☐ **Cloze.** Continue, by teaching *short e, short o,* and *short u* words:

1. When Mary was *bad*, she was sent to b_d.
     (bad → b_d → bed)

2. Harry took the *bat* and hoped he'd win the b_t.
     (bat → b_t → bet)

3. The *cat* meowed as she climbed over the c_t.
     (cat → c_t → cot)

4. The *map* was on the wall, the m_p on the floor.
     (map → m_p → mop)

5. John had no *hat* on his head when he climbed into the h_t.
     (hat → h_t → hut)

6. Pat tossed his *cap* and almost knocked over the c_p of coffee.
     (cap → c_p → cup)

Other pairs that could be used are:

a → e	a → o	a → u
man → men	bag → bog	bat → but
back → beck	cab → cob	back → buck
bag → beg	cap → cop	cab → cub
band → bend	flap → flop	cat → cut
Dan → den	Dan → Don	ham → hum
fad → fed	pad → pod	lamp → lump
sat → set	jab → job	mad → mud
land → lend	pat → pot	rat → rut
mash → mesh	rack → rock	sad → sud
mat → met	rat → rot	tag → tug
pack → peck	tap → top	snag → snug

☐ **Wet Cat.** Make a set of cards using cvc, cvcc, and ccvc words. Each pair of words has the same consonants but different vowels, e.g.: hat, hit; cap, cot; bed, bud; etc. Add an extra card— a Wet Cat. (Old Maid is no longer allowed.) Pupils draw from each other and make two-card books. Last child holding cards has the Wet Cat.

☐ **Sorting Pictures.** Cut out pictures from magazines. Each picture represents an object with a short vowel sound, e.g., rat, hit, bed, hut, mop, etc. Have children sort pictures into piles according to similar vowel sounds. Begin with just two different vowels; lead up to five.

Single
Vowels

☐ **Sorting Word Cards.** Do the same as above, but have words on the cards.

☐ **Solitaire.** Using 3 × 5" cards, make a deck using the words listed below. Children play like solitaire. There are *five suits*, according to vowel sounds, and in playing, the cards are arranged in alphabetical order by the first letter.

bad	bet	big	box	but
cat	cell	cid	cot	cup
dab	debt	did	dot	dud
fan	fez	fib	fond	fun
gas	gem	gin	got	gun
ham	hen	hit	hot	hum
jam	jet	jip	jot	jump
lap	let	lip	lot	lump
man	men	mid	mod	mud
nap	nest	nick	not	nut
pad	pet	pin	pod	pun
rag	red	rig	rod	run
sap	sex	sip	sob	sun
tab	ten	tip	top	tub

☐ **R Modified Vowels.** Put the following on the board:

_ar	_er	_ir	_or	_ur
ar_	er_	ir_	or_	ur_
_ar_	_er_	_ir_	_or_	_ur_
_ar	_er	_ir	_or	_ur
ar_	er_	ir_	or_	ur_
_ar_	_er_	_ir_	_or_	_ur_

Single Vowels

Have duplicates of each of the above in a hat.

1. Divide the class into two teams.
2. Play like "Spelldown," drawing a slip from the hat. The child whose turn it is must fill in the clozure(s) on the board, making a real word. For example, if you draw _ir_, the child might write in *dirt* or *bird*, etc.

☐ **Final** y = $/\bar{\imath}/$ or $/\bar{e}/$. Make cards using the following words:

long i: by, my, fry, try, cry, dry, spy, why, sly, sky, fly, pry

long e (short i): army, baby, berry, buggy, city, chilly, sunny, cooky, copy, cozy, daily, dandy, dolly, dusty, weedy, easy, empty, enemy, foxy, hobby, ivy, lily, woody, merry, plenty, ready, puppy, ruby, sleepy, sorry, story (others may be added).

1. Have the children who are playing sit in a circle. Count them off: 1, 2,—1, 2—1, 2, etc. One's are partners, and two's are partners.

2. Shuffle the deck, and deal the cards face down to the children. They keep the cards face down.

3. Children take turns in order. When a child has his turn, he turns up his top card. If he can pronounce the word and put it in the correct stack—one syllable word—two or more syllable word—he is rid of the card. If not, he puts the card on the bottom of the stack of his partner to his left.

4. The first team to be out of cards wins.

Single
Vowels

FINAL VOWEL-CONSONANT-E

☐ **Picture Sorting.** Mount pairs of pictures from magazines on cards. The following types of pairs might be used:

cap	– cape	fir	– fire
fin	– fine	glad	– glade
pet	– Pete	pan	– pane
cut	– cute	glob	– globe
hop	– hope	rip	– ripe
man	– mane	pin	– pine
can	– cane	tap	– tape
dim	– dime	van	– vane

Shuffle the cards and have a child sort them thus:

1. Short vowels in one stack, long vowels in another.
2. In books, e.g., cap and cape together; fin and fine together, etc.

☐ **Sentence Completion.** Pass out a ditto with sentences such as the following on it. Have children underline the correct word for each sentence.

1. The angry cat (spit, spite) at the dog.
2. The fruit was (rip, ripe) and ready to be eaten.
3. Marie found a (dim, dime) on the playground.
4. Janet brushed the horse's (man, mane).
5. Peter (cut, cute) his finger.

☐ **Which One?** Block off rectangles on a ditto master. Sketch a picture in each rectangle. If you're not artistic, just place an illustration over the ditto master sheet and trace, using a ball-point pen or stylus. Under the picture write two words—one with the final *e*, and the other without, thus:

rat	rate	fir	fire	pet	Pete	cub	cube	hop	hope

Have children circle the correct word. Give extra help to those children who have trouble.

☐ **Wet Cat.** Using 3 × 5" cards, make a deck by using some of the following pairs, besides those listed under the "Picture Sorting" activity in this section.

hat	– hate	rid	– ride
cut	– cute	rip	– ripe
bid	– bide	slid	– slide
hid	– hide	sit	– site
cop	– cope	sir	– sire
glob	– globe	snip	– snipe
her	– here	rat	– rate
mod	– mode	mad	– made
nod	– node	fad	– fade
purr	– pure	fat	– fate
grip	– gripe	bath	– bathe

Add a Wet Cat card. Play like Old Maid. To complete a book, the child must pronounce the two words correctly and use each in a sentence.

Final
v-c-*e*

VOWEL PAIRS

☐ **Sentence Completion.**   Pass out a ditto with sentences such as the following on it. Have children circle the correct answer.

1. Melvin hates to get out of _____ in the morning.
   bed   bead

2. Mary had a little lamb, but Harry had a _____.
   got   goat

3. Would you like a _____ hampster?
   pet   peat

4. Have you ever gone _____ digging?
   clam   claim

5. The mountain was _____.
   step   steep

☐ **Which One?**   Block off rectangles on a ditto master. Sketch a picture in each rectangle. Under the picture write two words, from which the child selects one, which is the name of the illustrated object. He circles the correct word. The following pairs might be used (at least one word in each pair is picturable):

man	–	main	mad	–	maid
am	–	aim	lad	–	laid
van	–	vain	far	–	fair
ran	–	rain	bet	–	beet
plan	–	plain	ten	–	teen
step	–	steep	cot	–	coat
met	–	meet	men	–	mean
fed	–	feed	pet	–	peat
rod	–	road	set	–	seat
got	–	goat	bet	–	beat

☐   **Quiet Pal Game.**   The teacher makes giant letter cards of the following types and pins one on each child: b, c, d, f, g, l, m, n, p, r, s, t, a, e, e, i, o. (Additional multiple copies of any of these letters, especially the vowels, can be used.)

1. The teacher then says a word, such as one of the following:

ran	fed	ten	plan
met	bed	pan	sped
cot	lest	bat	bran
pet	got	pep	bet
got	pad	rod	clam
pan	step	man	wed

2. The children who have the appropriate letters come to the front of the room to form the word, e.g.:

3. The teacher then asks for the vowel's Quiet Pal (in this case *a*'s Quiet Pal) to come to the front to form another word:

☐ **Crossword Pairs.** Make out a ditto master thus, and make enough copies so each child has one.

1. Ask the children to fill in silent vowel letters to make new words.

2. First child to complete this correctly wins.

or

1. Play like Bingo, with the teacher calling out the missing letter. (She has the letters on slips of paper and draws them from a hat.) The child writes in the letter when it is called.

2. First child to have his card completed correctly wins.

Follow-up

1. On the board, the teacher writes the words *man* and *van*. She asks a child to volunteer to use each in a sentence.

2. Then she writes *main* next to *man* and *vain* next to *van*. She asks for volunteers to use *main* and *vain* in sentences.

3. Then she asks a student to mark the vowels: a breve (⌣) above a short vowel, a macron (ˉ) above a long vowel, and a slash (/) through a silent vowel.

4. Continue, as above, with the other pairs.

☐   **Make Up a Story.** The teacher writes words such as the following on the board:

b*oi*l	bo*y*
sp*oi*l	co*y*
j*oi*n	to*y*
c*oi*n	vo*y*age
aster*oi*d	cowbo*y*
spher*oi*d	lo*y*al
p*oi*nsettia	jo*y*ous
p*oi*son	ro*y*al
av*oi*d	deco*y*

or

tr*ou*t	do*w*nfall
*ou*tlaw	gro*w*l
*ou*trage	pro*w*l
look*ou*t	cow*b*oy
b*ou*nd	po*w*der
b*ou*nty	do*w*dy
d*ou*bt	to*w*er
gr*ou*ch	glo*w*er
p*ou*t	vo*w*el

Together, the class makes up a story using as many of these words as possible.

☐   **Make Up Another Story.**   The teacher has words such as the following on separate cards:

ha*u*l	ba*w*l	b*all*
ha*u*nt	bra*w*l	c*all*
ma*u*l	ha*w*k	sm*all*
fa*u*n	fa*w*n	t*all*
ga*u*nt	ya*w*n	f*all*
s*au*cy	outla*w*	snowb*all*
*au*tumn	seesa*w*	waterf*all*
dino*sau*r	squa*w*	footb*all*
cent*au*r	tomaha*w*k	crestf*allen*

or

bab*oo*n	backw*oo*ds
ball*oo*n	w*oo*dshed
racc*oo*n	underf*oo*t
tr*oo*per	misunderst*oo*d
typh*oo*n	c*oo*k
pont*oo*n	br*oo*k
gl*oo*m	cr*oo*k
cr*oo*n	f*oo*tball
b*oo*m	fishh*oo*k

The cards are given to a child or a group of children to use in making up a story.

☐   **Ei or Ie?** *Ie* consistently represents a *long e* sound (sometimes called a *short i*) sound when it is in a final position; in other positions *ie* frequently represents the *long e* sound. *Ei* represents a *long a* sound, except when it follows a *c*. When *ei* follows a *c*, it frequently represents a *long e* sound. (Exceptions: sheik, either, neither, leisure, seisure.)

Children might learn the verse:

"*I* before *e* except after *c*
Or when sounded like *a*, as in *neighbor* and *weigh*. "

Write the following on the board:

	(omit)		(omit)		(omit)
f___ld	(ie)	r___ndeer	(ei)	gen___	(ie)
c ___ling	(ei)	gr___f	(ie)	y___ld	(ie)

sh__ld	(ie)	coll__	(ie)	bel__ve	(ie)
r__gn	(ei)	n__ghbor	(ei)	p__ce	(ie)
th__f	(ie)	dec__ve	(ei)	mov__	(ie)
n__ce	(ie)	ch__f	(ie)	w__gh	(ei)
conc__ve	(ei)	dec__t	(ei)	bel__f	(ie)
prair__	(ie)	v__l	(ei)	rec__pt	(ei)
p__r	(ie)	lass__	(ie)	eer__	(ie)
sk__n	(ei)	ach__ve	(ie)	b__ge	(ei)
f__rce	(ie)	ladd__	(ie)	rec__ve	(ei)
conc__t	(ei)	brown__	(ie)	f__nd	(ie)

1. Use a "Spelldown" technique, forming two teams in the class.
2. Draw from a hat $ei = /\bar{a}/$, $ei = /\bar{e}/$, or $ie = /\bar{e}/$. If you use the above list, you should have seven cards saying $ei = /\bar{a}/$, seven cards saying $ei = /\bar{e}/$, and 22 cards saying $ie = /\bar{e}/$.

To score a point for his team, the child must go to the board and insert the *ei* or *ie* in a proper place and use the word in a sentence.

☐ **Football.** The teacher draws a football field on the board, or better still, on the floor. She divides the class into two teams.

In a hat, the teacher has slips of paper, on each of which is one of the following vowel pairs: ai, ay, ea, ee, oa, ow, ou, oi, oy, oo, ei, ie. (Multiple copies of each pair are used.)

To remain on the offensive, a team must make ten yards in four attempts. If less yardage is made, the other side takes over. The game starts on the 50-yard line.

The team winning the toss is given four chances to make ten yards thus:

1. The teacher draws a vowel pair from the hat, and spells it to the first player.
2. The player scores two yards if he can name a word using that vowel pair. He scores an additional yard if he can use the word in a sentence, and one more yard if he can give a second word and also use it in a sentence. (During the total game, the same word cannot be used twice.)
3. The team retains possession of the ball when the third or fourth player has completed ten or more yards for his team and finishes his turn. Then another first down is

begun. If four consecutive players do not complete ten or more yards, the opposing team takes over, heading toward its opponent's goal.

4. A touchdown is made when a team reaches its opponent's goal line. The team scores six points for a touchdown. Following this, a field goal, worth one point, is scored if the next player earns four yards.

5. After a touchdown is made and the field goal is attempted, the opposing team takes over on the 50-yard line.

6. Total playing time is determined before the game begins. The team having the highest score at the end of the time period wins.

Vowel Pairs

SYLLABICATION

☐ **Name Game (Auditory).** Ask children to stand up in the following order:

1. Those who have one syllable in their first names. Ask the children to say their names out loud, then sit down.
2. Those who have two syllables in their first names. Proceed as before.
3. Those who have three syllables in their first names. Proceed as before. Continue with four syllables, etc.
4. Do the same with last names.
5. Do the same with total syllables in first plus last names.

☐ **Name Game (Visual).** Ask children to write their names on the board and to circle vowel graphemes in their names in the same order as above. One, and only one vowel grapheme is circled for each syllable, for example:

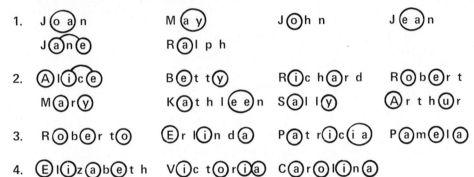

1. J (o a) n   M (a y)   J (o) h n   J (e a) n
   J (a) n (e)   R (a) l p h

2. (A) l (i) c (e)   B (e) t t (y)   R (i) c h (a) r d   R (o) b (e) r t
   M (a) r (y)   K (a) t h l (e e) n   S (a) l l (y)   (A) r t h (u) r

3. R (o) b (e) r t (o)   (E) r l (i) n d (a)   P (a) t r (i) c (i a)   P (a) m (e) l (a)

4. (E) l (i) z (a) b (e) t h   V (i) c t (o) r (i a)   c (a) r (o) l (i) n (a)

☐ **Card Sorting.** Make a set of 3 × 5" cards with a *hypothetical word* on each one. Ask students to sort cards according to the number of syllables in the word. This must follow a thorough explanation in class.

v = vowel, c = consonant, l = l, e = e

One syllable	Two syllables	Three syllables
c v	c v c v c	v v c v v c v c
c v c	v v c v c	v c v v c l e
c c v c	c v c l e	v c v c v l e
c v v	c v v c c l e	c c v c v c c v v
c v v c	c v c v c e	v c v c v c e

One syllable	Two syllables	Three syllables
v c e	v c v c	c v c c v c l e
c v c e	c c v c c v	v v c c v v c c v
c v v c e	v v c v v	c v c v c v c

Be sure to explain when errors have been made.

☐   **Card Sorting.** Make a set of 3 X 5" cards with a nonsense word on each. Ask students to sort cards according to the number of syllables in the word. This must follow a thorough explanation in class. For example:

one syllable	two syllables	three syllables
e m	a i s e m p	b e i s r o o d l e
a m e	d e i s a y	k o u g g e r t e n e
s a i m	t o a d d l e	a w f m e i g a
d e e	m e i n g e t	u m p o r t o
p e k	o o g e m p	s e j o r t e e
s y	k e d y	n o o r t e e d a y
t o d e	m a u s e y	e a z a r p a f e
e e t	p e a r e d e	k o o m i s t l e

Be sure to explain when errors have been made.

☐   **Card Sorting.** Use real words.

☐   **Wet Cat.** Use the cards prepared for the three card sorting activities above, or any combination of these. Add a Wet Cat card. Play like Old Maid, with three cards to a book: three hypothetical words, one with one syllable, one with two, one with three—or three nonsense words, or three real words.

Variation. Books of two cards each: e.g., two "hypothetical words" or two nonsense words, or two real words, each with the same number of syllables.

☐   **Dart Game.** Make a dart board using concentric circles, thus:

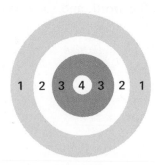

Darts can be used, or the board could be laid on the floor and tokens can be tossed. If the dart or token lands in number 4, the child must give a four-syllable word, and for this he scores four points. He gives a three-syllable word if it lands in number 3, and for this he scores three points. Etc. Individuals or teams may play.

☐ **Syllabication (vccv).** Teach the following generalization inductively, "When two vowel sounds (or graphemes) are separated by two consonants, divide between the consonants," thus:

1. List words such as the following on the board:

organ	turban	tender	hornet
altar	forget	marvel	fancy
shoulder	alto	sentence	service
mascot	pasture	tablet	bamboo
public	hasty	aspen	number

2. Say a sentence which would include one of these words. Ask the children to supply the word, for example:

   a) "I hope I won't _____ to do my homework. Yes, *forget* is the word . . . Say it. Where do we syllabicate? Yes, between the two consonants." Write the board:

      for - get
      vc - cv

   b) Continue with enough examples until the children can tell you the generalization.

   c) Then give them other examples to see if they can do them on their own.

☐ **Context Clues.** Ask children to look at one page in a book they are reading and from that page to select all words that have a vccv pattern. They should read the sentence in which each of these words is found, write the word, and show where it is divided into syllables.

☐ **Syllabication (vcv).** Do the same as above, but using examples such as the following:

(v/cv)		(vc/v)	
notice	razor	habit	olive
legal	deny	river	cover

(v/cv)		(vc/v)	
nomad	*eth*er	digit	panic
digest	cigar	*eth*ics	honor
sonar	hazy	avid	diner
paper	platoon	credit	jaguar

```
no - tice      _____      hab - it       _____
 v -  cv                         vc  - v

le - gal       _____      riv - er       _____
 v -  cv                         vc  - v

no - mad       _____      dig - it       _____
 v -  cv                         vc  - v

etc.           _____      etc.           _____
```

The generalization to be induced is: "When two vowel sounds (or graphemes) are separated by one consonant, divide before consonant or after it." Try one way—if you don't recognize the word, try the other way.

☐   **Syllabication (-cle).** Continue in the same way, using words such as:

cable	table	maple	eagle	dimple
handle	uncle	poodle	mingle	gamble
rumble	mantle	hurdle	fable	cycle

```
ca - ble    _____  _____  _____  _____
   - cle

han - dle   _____  _____  _____  _____
    - cle

rum - ble   _____  _____  _____  _____
    - cle
```

Syllabication

The generalization is: "When a word ends in consonant-*l-e*, divide before the consonant."

☐ **Picture Clues.** The teacher collects a set of pictures representing two- or three-syllable words. Each picture is pasted on a card, and the word, in part, is written under the picture, with one or more consonants clozed, e.g.:

wi_dow

de_il

sta_le

ra_or

The child writes the complete word and shows where it is divided into syllables.

☐ **Save the Drowning Child.** On a large chart the teacher has a picture of a child in swimming calling for help. She has an equal number of pockets leading to the child from two directions, and two pictures of lifeguards.

1. The class is divided into two teams.
2. The teacher holds up a card with a word on it.
3. In relay fashion, one person from each team runs to the board to write the word and show where it is divided into syllables. (Even one-syllable words can be used to show that no division is made.)
4. The child who is first to divide the word properly is asked to use the word in a sentence. If he can, he scores for his team, and the lifeguard representing his team is moved one pocket closer to the drowning child.
5. The team whose lifeguard reaches the child first wins.

Syllabication

☐   **Haiku.** Students may enjoy composing a Japanese form of verse called haiku. These unrhymed poems reflect a mood, are *usually* about nature, often depict or suggest a season of the year, and are brief. They consist of three lines only, with a total of seventeen syllables.[2] Lines one and three each contain five syllables, and line two has seven syllables. For example:

Syllabication

_____

[2] You may wish to see the film "Making Haiku" by Anette Klingman. It is a 16 mm sound film that runs for eight minutes: No. 3119 from Encyclopoedia Britannica Educational Corp., 425 N. Michigan Ave., Chicago, Illinois 60611.

Snow falls like feathers
On the coldest winter night
And covers the world.   Teresa Mattix

White paws and black tail
Sparkling eyes through darkness
Pink nose wet with love.   Iris Morgenstern

Six in the covey
On our picket garden fence
Bob whites in a row.   L. B.

☐   **Quinzaine** (kăn zĕn′).   Another verse form youngsters might enjoy is quinzaine. A quinzaine has three lines with a total of 15 syllables. Line one, composed of seven syllables, is a statement. Lines two and three are in question form and are composed of five and three syllables, respectively. For example:

Michelle is poised for battle.
Will she demolish
Catnip Mouse?   L. B.

Juniper boughs are swaying.
What makes them dance so,
Rolling wind?   Ignacio Montoya

☐   **Quintain** (kwĭn ten′).   Students also enjoy composing verses in syllabic progression. A quintain has five lines with two syllables in line one, four syllables in line two, six in line three, eight in line four, and ten in line five. For example:

The sun
Sets on the tops
Of hills while birds sing songs.
It's nice to live in a clean world
With people who are proud to dwell in it.   Albert Silva

People
Walking swiftly
Always in a hurry—
Not even knowing where to go
Trying to get away from their despair.   John Heddlesten

Syllabication

Silent Consonants

SILENT CONSONANTS

Appendix A

Two unlike consonant letters are sometimes used to represent one consonant sound. Only those are listed which occurred six or more times in Hanna's 17,310 words.[1]

grapheme	phoneme	examples	position in syllable	number of instances in 17,310 words
bt	t	debt, doubt	final	11
dg	j	dodge, bridge	final	51
dj	j	a-djust	initial	13
gh	f	e-nough, laugh	final	8
gh	g	ghost, ghastly	initial	9
		burgh	final	1
gn	n	gnat, gnome	initial	5
		sign, reign	final	27
kn	n	kneel, knot	initial	37

[1] Lou E. Burmeister, "Content of a Phonics Program Based on Particularly Useful Generalizations," In Nila Banton Smith (editor), *Reading Methods and Teacher Improvement*, Newark, Del.: International Reading Association, 1971, p. 34. Used by permission of the International Reading Association.

grapheme	phoneme	examples	position in syllable	number of instances in 17,310 words
lm	m	a-lmond	initial	2
		alms	medial	2
		calm, palm	final	13
lk	k	chalk, talk	final	14
mb	m	bomb, comb	final	27
mn	m	hymn, autumn	final	7
rh	r	rhyme, rhetoric	initial	16
ps	s	psalm, pseudo	initial	19
tch	ch	catch, witch	final	61
wh	h	who, whole	initial	12
wr	r	wrap, write	initial	48

Silent Consonants

Single Vowels

Frequency and percent of occurrence of each phoneme for each single-vowel grapheme according to syllabic position and accent pattern. All single vowels which occurred in Hanna's 17,310 words are included in total (Σ) listings, but only the most frequently occurring sounds are described.[1] (See p. 134.)

Single
Vowels

---

[1] Lou E. Burmeister, "The Effect of Syllabic Position and Accent Pattern on the Phonemic Behavior of Single Vowel Graphemes," in J. Allen Figurel (editor), *Reading and Realism*, Newark, Del.: International Reading Association, 1969, p. 648. Used by permission of the International Reading Association.

grapheme	phoneme	example	Open syllable Total f %	Accented f %	Unaccented f %	Closed syllable Total f %	Accented f %	Unaccented f %
a	ā	halo	860 32.4	849 93.0	11 .6	142 2.8	139 4.1	3 .2
a	â	vary	0 0	0 0	0 0	64 1.3	64 1.9	0 0
a	ă	baboon	304 11.5	1 .1	303 17.4	3888 76.6	2485 73.4	1403 82.7
a	ä	arm	58 2.2	49 5.4	9 .5	460 9.1	383 11.3	77 4.5
a	ə	canal	1418 53.4	0 0	1418 81.5	19 .4	0 0	19 1.1
Σa			2654	913	1741	5078	3382	1696
e	ē	senior	1740 90.4	345 97.7	1395 88.8	25 .4	18 .6	7 .2
e	e̦	hero	0 0	0 0	0 0	64 1.0	63 2.2	1 .03
e	ĕ	bet	44 2.3	1 .3	43 2.7	3272 48.3	2419 85.2	853 21.7
e	ẽ	after	6 .3	1 .3	5 .3	1660 24.5	0 0	1660 42.2
e	ə	angel	115 6.0	0 0	115 7.3	648 9.6	1 .04	647 16.5
e	û	her	0 0	0 0	0 0	313 4.6	288 10.1	25 .6
le	'l	able	0 0	0 0	0 0	620 9.2	0 0	620 15.8
Σe			1924	353	1571	6772	2840	3932
i	ī	china	395 14.2	294 94.8	101 4.1	159 3.4	158 5.7	1 .1
i	ĭ	in	1039 37.3	0 0	1039 41.9	4307 91.5	2417 86.9	1890 98.0
i	ə	pencil	1332 47.8	0 0	1332 53.7	15 .3	0 0	15 .8
i	ē	ski	23 .8	16 5.2	7 .3	15 .3	13 .5	2 .1
Σi			2789	310	2479	4709	2781	1928
o	ō	so	1629 92.0	545 97.0	1084 89.7	247 5.8	208 9.5	39 1.9
o	ô	cord	0 0	0 0	0 0	312 7.4	262 12.0	50 2.4
o	ŏ	dot	0 0	0 0	0 0	1557 36.7	1425 65.0	132 6.4
o	ô̇	off	0 0	0 0	0 0	123 2.9	102 4.7	21 1.0
o	ə	carton	114 6.4	0 0	114 9.4	1497 35.3	0 0	1497 73.0
o	õ	humor	0 0	0 0	0 0	268 6.3	0 0	268 13.1
o	ŭ	son	0 0	0 0	0 0	112 2.6	110 5.0	2 .1
Σo			1770	562	1208	4243	2192	2051
u	ū	union	770 82.6	320 82.3	450 82.0	44 2.3	29 2.3	15 2.3
u	û	burn	0 0	0 0	0 0	203 10.6	188 14.7	15 2.3
u	ũ	cup	2 .2	0 0	2 .4	1210 62.9	996 77.8	214 33.3
u	ə	submit	42 4.5	0 0	42 7.7	255 13.3	0 0	255 39.7
u	o͞o	truth	82 8.8	69 17.7	13 2.4	11 .6	11 .9	0 0
u	o͝o	put	36 3.9	0 0	36 6.6	164 8.6	51 4.0	113 17.6
Σu			932	389	543	1923	1280	643

Vowel Pairs

Appendix C

Frequency and percent of occurrence of each phoneme for each single vowel-pair grapheme in the Hanna, *et. al.*, list of the 17,310 most common English words.[1]

Grapheme			Phonemic behavior		
Name	Frequency	Pronun-ciation key	Example	Frequency	Percent (%)
first vowel long, second vowel silent					
ai	(309)	ā	abstain	230	74.4
		â	air	49	15.5
		ĭ	mountain	15	4.9
		ə	villain	9	2.9
		ĕ	again	4	1.3
		ă	plaid	1	.3
		ī	aisle	1	.3

Vowel
Pairs

---

[1] Lou E. Burmeister, "Vowel Pairs," *The Reading Teacher* 21 (February 1968): 448–449. Used by permission of the International Reading Association.

Grapheme			Phonemic behavior		
Name	Frequency	Pronun-ciation key	Example	Frequency	Percent %
ay	(137)	$\bar{a}$	gray	132	96.4
		$\bar{i}$	kayak	3	2.2
		$\breve{e}$	says	1	.7
		ĭ	yesterday	1	.7
ea	(545)	$\bar{e}$	east	275	50.5
		$\breve{e}$	weapon	140	25.7
		$\bar{e}_\backslash$	ear	49	9.0
		û	earth	31	5.7
		â	bear	13	2.4
		ä	hearty	18	3.3
		$\bar{a}$	great	14	2.6
		ĭ	guinea	2	.4
		ə	sergeant	3	.5
ee	(290)	$\bar{e}$	sleet	248	85.5
		$\bar{e}_\backslash$	peer	36	12.4
		ĭ	been	6	2.1
ey	(69)	ĭ[2]	honey	40	58.0
		$\bar{a}$	convey	14	20.3
		$\bar{i}$	geyser	8	11.6
		$\bar{e}$	key	6	8.7
		â	eyrie	1	1.4
oa	(138)	$\bar{o}$	road	129	93.5
		ô	broad	9	6.5
ow	(250)	$\bar{o}$	own	125	50.0
		ou	town	121	48.4
		ŏ	knowledge	4	1.6

Vowel Pairs

diphthongs					
oi	(102)	oi	moist	100	98.0
		ə	porpoise	2	2.0
oy	(50)	oi	convoy	49	98.0
		$\bar{i}$	coyote	1	2.0
ou	(803)	ə	rigorous	336	41.2
		ou	out	285	35.0
		$\overline{oo}$	soup	54	6.6

---

[2] reclassified long e (e)

Grapheme			Phonemic behavior		
Name	Frequency	Pronun- ciation key	Example	Frequency	Percent %
		ō	four	47	5.8
		ŭ	touch	30	3.7
		o͞o	your	25	3.1
		û	journey	22	2.7
		ĕ	glamour	1	.1
ow	(250)	ō	own	125	50.0
		ou	town	121	48.4
		ŏ	knowledge	4	1.6
broad a (ô)					
au	(178)	ô	auction	167	93.8
		ō	chauffeur	5	2.8
		ä	laugh	4	2.2
		ə	epaulet	1	.6
		ā	gauge	1	.6
aw	(77)	ô	lawn	77	100
long and short oo					
oo	(315)	o͞o	lagoon	185	58.7
		o͝o	wood	114	36.2
		ō	floor	9	2.9
		ŭ	blood	7	2.2
ei and ie					
ei	(86)	ā	reign	34	40.0
		ē	deceit	22	25.6
		ĭ	foreign	11	12.8
		ī	seismic	9	10.5
		â	their	5	5.8
		ə	sovereignty	2	2.3
		ē̦	weird	2	2.3
		ĕ	heifer	1	1.2
ie	(156)	ē	thief	56	35.9
		ĭ[3]	lassie	30	19.2
		ī	die	26	16.7

---

[3] reclassified long e (ē)

Grapheme		Phonemic behavior			
Name	Frequency	Pronunciation key	Example	Frequency	Percent %
		ə	patient	23	14.7
		$\overline{e}$	cashier	17	10.9
		e	friend	4	2.6

miscellaneous and rare combinations

ae	(6)	$\overline{e}$	algae	5	83.3
		ĕ	aesthetic	1	16.7
ao	(2)	ô	extraordinary	2	100
eo	(15)	ə	pigeon	10	66.7
		ĕ	leopard	3	20.0
		$\overline{e}$	people	2	13.3
eu	(40)	$\overline{u}$	feud	29	72.5
		û	amateur	6	15.0
		$\overline{oo}$	sleuth	4	10.0
		ŏŏ	pleurisy	1	2.5
ew	(64)	$\overline{u}$	news	39	60.9
		$\overline{oo}$	flew	22	34.4
		$\overline{o}$	sew	3	4.7
ia	(5)	ĭ	carriage	3	60
		ə	parliament	2	40
oe	(22)	$\overline{o}$	foe	13	59.1
		$\overline{e}$	amoeba	5	22.7
		$\overline{oo}$	shoe	4	18.2
ue	(43)	$\overline{u}$	due, cue	27	62.8
		$\overline{oo}$	clue	16	37.2
ui	(34)	ĭ	build	16	47.1
		$\overline{oo}$	fruit	10	29.4
		$\overline{u}$	suit	8	23.5
uo	(2)	$\overline{oo}$	buoyant	2	100
uy	(3)	$\overline{i}$	buy	3	100

Vowel
Pairs

Some Phonics Programs

Brake, Rachel G. *New Phonics Skilltext.* Columbus, Ohio: Charles E. Merrill, 1964.

Clymer, Theodore, and Thomas C. Barrett and Lou E. Burmeister. *Ginn Word Enrichment Program.* Boston, Mass.: Ginn, 1968, 1972.

Durrell, Donald D., and Helen A. Murphy. *Phonics Practice Program*, also, *Speech-to-Print Phonics: a Phonics Foundation for Reading.* New York: Harcourt, Brace, Jovanovich, 1968, 1964.

Harris, Theordore L., and Mildred Creekmore and Margaret Greenman. *Phonetic Keys to Reading* (grades 1-3) and *Keys to Independence in Reading* (grades 4-6). Oklahoma City, Okla.: The Economy Co., 1971.

Helmkamp, Ruth, and Aileen Thomas. *Phonics We Use.* Chicago, Ill.: Lyons and Carnahan, 1966.

Rice, Charles. *Phonics Transparencies.* Wilkensbury; Pa.: Hayes School Publishing Co., 1968.

Ryan, Isabella Bayne. *Phonics and Word-Analysis Skills.* Elizabethtown, N.J.: Continental Press, 1967.

Stone, Clarence. *Phonics Workbooks.* New York: Webster Division, McGraw Hill, 1971.

Sullivan, M.W. *The Sullivan Reading Program.* Palo Alto, Calif.: Behavioral Research Laboratories, 1973.

The scope of many commercial phonics programs in popular use today is fairly standard; but the sequence, or order, of the

Programs

presentation of generalizations varies to some extent. However, a fairly typical sequential pattern is:

Readiness

1. visual discrimination of letters and words
2. auditory discrimination of rhyming sounds in words and of initial consonant sounds in words
3. visual-motor coordination for writing letters and words

Reading. Grapheme to phoneme relationships, or perhaps phoneme to grapheme relationships for:

1. *single consonants* - in initial and final positions and medial positions
2. *single vowels* - in closed syllables - short sound
3. *consonant digraphs and blends*
4. *final vowel-consonant-e*
5. *single vowels* in open and closed syllables, the *schwa* and *r control*
6. *common vowel pairs* – *ai, ay, ee, ea, oa, ow;*
   oi, oy, ou, ow diphthongs;
   oo, also *au, aw,* also *ei, ie*
7. *c and g generalizations; silent consonants*
8. *syllabication*

Possible Sequential Patterns for Teaching Word Analysis Skills

POSSIBLE SEQUENTIAL PATTERN FOR
TEACHING WORD ANALYSIS SKILLS

Grade	Sight Vocabulary
K	Recognizes own name in print Recognizes likenesses and differences in letters, words, and numbers Can match capital and lower case letters Recognizes basic colors, sizes, and shapes Uses some configuration clues to words
1	Recognizes whether words begin with capital or lower case letters Learns number words from zero to ten, and arabics Learns basic color words Learns words frequently seen on TV Learns the major holidays Learns opposites such as stop go, off on Learns 110 words on Dolch list and/or first grade words on Fry's list of "Instant Words" and/or most basal reader words
2	Learns number words to twenty, the days of the week, and the months Learns common contractions formed with verb + not, such as don't, won't, isn't, aren't Learns most of the additional words on Dolch list and/or second grade words on Fry's list and/or most basal reader words

Grade | Sight Vocabulary

Grade	Sight Vocabulary
3	Learns all common contractions, such as I've, he'd, you'll Learns simple prefixes and suffixes Learns basic abbreviations: A.M., P.M., Ave., St., days and months Learns all remaining Dolch list words and/or Fry list words and/or most basal reader words Continues transferring words to sight vocabulary after recognizing them through another mode
4 5 6	Learns Roman numerals Recognizes common prefixes and suffixes Continues to transfer words to sight vocabulary through wide reading
7-12	Recognizes all basic words and phrases commonly used at grade level in all subjects Learns technical abbreviations Continues to transfer new words to sight vocabulary through wide and in-depth reading Eye-span for sight recognition reaches phrase length

Grade	Context Clues
K	Is able to classify, e.g., animals, foods, shapes, colors, sizes Is able to sequence picture cards Is able to tell a story in his own words and to anticipate endings
1	Recognizes word labels on objects and pictures Is able to classify words with appropriate objects and pictures Given a sentence of a common pattern, is able to substitute appropriate words in a clozure Given a sentence, is able to substitute words keeping one or more phonic elements stable Is able to combine context and phonics in word recognition Is able to use past experience in learning
2	Gains in versatility in combining the use of context clues and phonics in word recognition Recognizes the appropriate meaning of a word to fit context Is able to make associations, such as "sun shines", "rain falls" Recognizes that a change in intonation changes meaning Given a sentence, is able to add simple elaborations when prompted

Grade	Context Clues
3	Recognizes that words have multiple meanings Develops vocabulary by using synonyms, antonyms Gains skill in recognizing and using words connotatively Begins to recognize literary uses of language: similies, metaphors, personification, simple allusions Uses punctuation as a cue to meaning Gains in proficiency in convergently and divergently classifying words Is able to pick out relevant and irrelevant ideas in classifying
4 5 6	Continues to grow in areas listed above Uses sentence structure as a clue to meaning, especially appositives, examples, restatements, definitions, and contrasts Uses phrase and clause signal words, or markers, as clues to word recognition and meaning Recognizes idioms and clichés Uses maps, pictures, graphs, and other illustrations as clues to meaning
7-12	Uses clues of the following types to arrive at meaning: definition and explanation, synonyms or restatement of meaning, comparison and contrast, example, summary, experience, reflection of a mood or situation, anticipation Continues growing in ability to use illustrations: maps, graphs, charts, pictures Grows in the appreciation of language diversity (dialects) Grows in the use and understanding of figurative language Grows in the ability to convergently and divergently classify words and concepts Grows in the understanding of semantics and rhetoric

Grade	Morphology
K	Orally recognizes simple compound words, e.g., mailman, milkman Orally recognizes the use of simple sequence words: first, last, before, next, over, under Recognizes and uses the variant ending "s" with nouns or verbs, when appropriate
1	Learns the variant endings: -s, -es, -ed, -ing Learns abbreviations: Mr. and Mrs. Learns single possessives and some simple contractions Learns additional compound words, e.g., oatmeal, bluebird

Grade	Morphology
2	Learns plural possessives Begins combining simple bound morphemes with free English morphemes, e.g., *un*kind, *re*makes, thought*ful*, *dis*loyal, *in*laid Learns the variant endings -er, -ly, -fully Continues growing in the use of contractions, e.g., isn't, aren't, wasn't, don't Is introduced to morphological syllabication
3	Learns the meanings for common prefixes: un, re, dis, in, pre, super, sub, co Learns the uses of common suffixes: -er, -est, -ful, -less Learns morphological syllabication generalizations: prefix/root; root/root; root/suffix
4 5 6	Begins combining two bound morphemes: geography, biology, etc. Recognizes simple Greek and Latin morphemes and their meanings, e.g., uni, mono, bi, tri, quad, and other number morphemes as well as others Extends knowledge of prefixes, suffixes, compound words, contractions, and comparatives Extends use of abbreviations Learns common blends, e.g., brunch, smog, etc. Learns common acronyms
7-12	Extends use of prefixes, suffixes, and roots to include technical words in the content areas Learns something about the changing nature of language and that new words constantly find their way into English through new combinations of morphemes (aquanaut, cosmonaut), blending (motel, skort), acronyms (NATO, scuba), borrowing (sputnik, taco), etc., and also that meanings of words change (criticize, propaganda, villain, etc.)

Grade	Phonic Analysis
K	Is able to identify sounds in the immediate environment Learns the alphabet (basis for phonics) Learns to auditorily discriminate words that rhyme Learns to auditorily discriminate initial consonants Is able to sort pictures according to rhyming sounds or initial consonants Is aware that there is a relationship between the printed word and the sound it represents

Grade	Phonic Analysis
1	Learns phoneme-grapheme (or grapheme-phoneme) relationships for: a) initial consonants and consonant blends of the families -r, -l, s- b) common final consonant clusters c) short vowels in closed syllables of the cvc pattern, e.g., cap, pet, bit, hop, cut d) consonant digraphs: ch, sh, th, ph, ng Combines the use of phonics with context clues
2	Learns phoneme-grapheme (or grapheme-phoneme) relationships for: a) long vowels in the cvce patterns, e.g., cape, Pete, bite, hope, cute b) the following vowel pairs: ai, ay, ee, ea, oa, ow (digraphs) c) "r-modified" vowels, e.g., car, care, her, here, fir, fire, for, fore, hurt d) the two sounds of c and g e) three sounds of y (yes, my, baby) f) the following vowel pairs: ou, ow; oi, oy (dipthongs), and the two sounds represented by oo Is introduced to the schwa sound Is introduced to syllabication of two-syllable words in the patterns: vc/cv (for/mer), v/cv (ra/zor), vc/v (lem/on) Combines the use of phonics with context clues
3	Learns phoneme-grapheme (or grapheme-phoneme) relationships for: a) the vowel pairs: au, aw (broad a, or circumflex o) and ei, ie b) the "consonantizing of i," especially in suffixes: cion, tion, sion Continues to refine syllabication skills in the patterns vccv, vcv, and learns the final -cle generalization Is aware of stress in polysyllabic words Combines the use of phonics with context clues
4 5 6	Is taught phonics concepts which he failed to learn earlier All phonic concepts are reinforced, especially the c and g generalizations, phonic syllabication, and vowel pairs Stress is placed on combining phonic analysis with context clues and morphology
7-12	Same as above Teaching is diagnostic

References for Further Reading

Bailey, Mildred Hart. "The Utility of Phonic Generalizations in Grades One through Six." *The Reading Teacher* 20 (February 1967): 413–418.

Bloomfield, Leonard and C. Barnhart. *Let's Read: A Linguistic Approach.* Detroit, Mich.: Wayne State University Press, 1961.

Burmeister, Lou E. "The Usefulness of Phonic Generalizations." *The Reading Teacher* 21 (January 1968): 349–364+.

_____. "Vowel Pairs." *The Reading Teacher* 21 (February 1968): 445–452.

_____. "Selected Word Analysis Generalizations for a Group Approach to Corrective Reading in the Secondary School." *Reading Research Quarterly* IV (Fall 1968): 71-95.

_____. "Final Vowel-Consonant-*e*." *The Reading Teacher* 24 (February 1971): 439–442.

_____. "The Effect of Syllabic Position and Accent Pattern on the Phonemic Behavior of Single Vowel Graphemes." *Reading and Realism.* Newark, Del.: IRA, 1969, 645–649.

_____. "Content of a Phonics Program Based on Particularly Useful Generalizations." *Reading Methods and Teacher Improvement,* Nila B. Smith (editor). Newark, Del.: IRA, 1971.

_____ and Thaddeus Trela. "Phonic Syllabication in the v c v Pattern," in progress.

Clymer, Theodore L. "The Utility of Phonic Generalizations in the Primary Grades." *The Reading Teacher* 16 (January 1963): 252–258.

Dawson, Mildred (editor). *Teaching Word Recognition Skills.* Newark, Del.: International Reading Association, 1971.

Dulin, Kenneth L. "New Research on Context Clues." *The Journal of Reading* 13 (1969): 33–38.

Emans, Robert. "The Usefulness of Phonic Generalizations above the Primary Grades." *The Reading Teacher* **20** (February 1967): 419–425.

Fries, C. C. *Linguistics and Reading.* New York: Holt, Rinehart and Winston, 1963.

Heilman, Arthur. *Phonics in Proper Perspective.* Columbus, Ohio: Charles E. Merrill Books, 1968.

Lefevre, Carl A. *Linguistics and the Teaching of Reading.* New York: McGraw-Hill Book Co., 1964.

_____. "The Simplistic Standard Word-Perception Theory of Reading." *Elementary English* **45** (1968): 349–353.

Smith, H. L., Jr. *English Morphophonics: Implications for the Teaching of Literacy.* SUNY at Oneonta, New York: New York State English Council, 1968.

Trela, Thaddeus. *Fourteen Remedial Reading Methods.* Belmont, Calif.: Fearon Publishers, 1968.

Answers

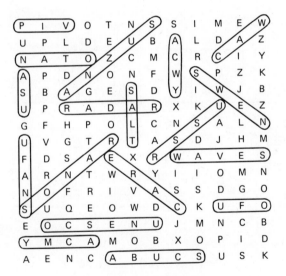

Acronym search

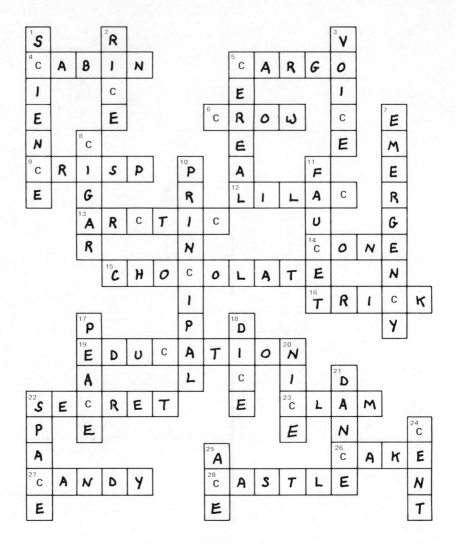

Crossword puzzle: C

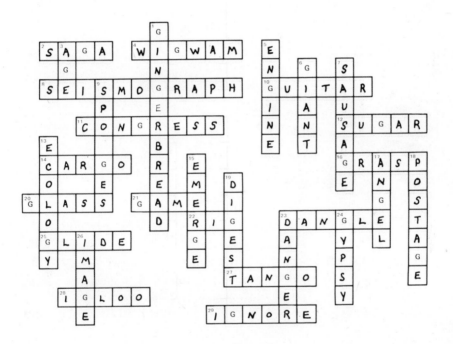

Crossword puzzle: G

Index